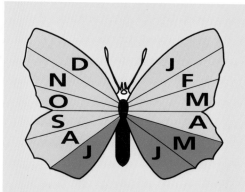

Butterfly
Flight Periods

One of these symbols is shown with
each species entry. It shows you
at a glance the period or periods
when this butterfly is in flight.
This is the time of year when you
are mostly like to see one.

BUTTERFLIES
OF GREAT BRITAIN & EUROPE

CONSULTANT
Dr George C. McGavin

EDITED BY
Susan McKeever

ILLUSTRATIONS BY
Brian Hargreaves

DRAGON'S WORLD

CHILDREN'S BOOKS

Conservation

Over 15,000 species of butterfly live on Earth and there are just over 400 different butterflies to be found in Great Britain and Europe. Most insects live in the tropics, and over half of them live in tropical rain forests. Many butterflies also live in wetlands – like flood plains, marshes and swamps.

Unfortunately these two habitats are the ones that are most at risk in the world today. People are felling the tropical rain forests for the hardwoods, like mahogany, to make furniture, or clearing them for farms. People are draining wetlands because they are good places to farm once the water has gone. Either way, unique butterfly species are being lost every week.

On page 78 you will find the names of some organizations who campaign for the protection of particular animals and habitats in Great Britain and around the world. By joining them and supporting their efforts, **you** can help to preserve our wildlife.

Butterfly Hunter's Code

1 **Always go collecting with a friend,** and always tell an adult where you have gone.
2 **Treat all butterflies with care** – they are delicate creatures and can be easily killed by rough handling.
3 **Ask permission** before exploring or crossing private property.
5 **Keep to footpaths** as much as possible.
6 **Keep off crops and leave fence gates** as you find them.
7 **Ask your parents not to light fires** except in fire places in special picnic areas.
8 **Take your litter home.**

Dragon's World Ltd
Limpsfield
Surrey RH8 0DY
Great Britain

Published by Dragon's World
in Great Britain, 1995

© Dragon's World, 1995
© Text Dragon's World, 1995
© Species illustrations Brian Hargreaves, 1991 & 1995
© Other illustrations Dragon's World, 1995

All rights reserved

Simplified text and captions by Susan McKeever, based on *Butterflies of Britain and Europe* by John Feltwell.

Habitat paintings by Michael Saunders. Headbands by Antonia Phillips. Identification and activities illustrations by Mr Gay Galsworthy.

Editor	Diana Briscoe
Designer	James Lawrence
Design Assistants	Karen Ferguson
	Victoria Furbisher
Art Director	John Strange
Editorial Director	Pippa Rubinstein

ISBN 1 85028 293 5

Typeset in Frutiger Light and Novarese Bold by Dragon's World Ltd.
Printed in Slovenia

Contents

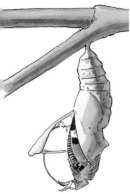

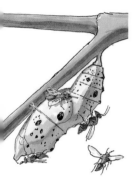

What Is a Butterfly?

Fluttering butterflies live everywhere in Europe. You can spot them in a huge variety of places – on mountains, in damp bogs, in sunny woodlands, flying through meadows, and in your own back garden. You already know that they are beautiful to look at, but they also have a fascinating lifestyle.

This book will help you to become a butterfly spotter in two ways. It only shows you the butterflies that you are most likely to see, and it puts them in the habitat, or type of countryside, where you are most likely to see them.

Where butterflies choose to live depends a lot on the flowers and plants they like to feed on. So knowing a butterfly's favourite plant, and where it grows, is a great help toward knowing where to spot that butterfly.

The life of a butterfly

Butterflies go through four very different stages in their lives, and you can look for them at each stage. The first stage is the egg. Next comes the caterpillar, the chrysalis, and finally the butterfly.

Changing from one form to another like this is called complete metamorphosis (change in form) because the larval (young) stages are completely different from the adult.

The caterpillar hatches (it eats its way out of the egg) and immediately starts to feed on the food plant. As it grows larger, it has to moult (shed its skin) because caterpillar skins cannot stretch.

The female butterfly lays her eggs on the plant that she knows her caterpillar likes to eat.

After shedding its skin for the last time, the caterpillar finds a twig where it can turn into a chrysalis. It spins a silken pad from which the chrysalis hangs.

How to use this book

To identify a butterfly you don't recognize, like the two shown here, follow these steps.

1 **Draw a quick sketch of the butterfly** (see page 23) in your field notebook. Draw the outline first, then fill in any other features you notice. Write down where and when you spotted the butterfly.

2 **Decide what habitat you are in.** If you read the descriptions at the start of each section, you'll soon see which one fits where you are. Each habitat has a different picture band.

3 **Look through the section with this picture band.** The picture and information given for each butterfly will help you identify it. The brightly patterned butterfly shown to the right is a Peacock (see page 14).

4 **If you can't find the butterfly there,** look through the other sections. Some butterflies can live in a big variety of habitats.

5 **Sometimes, the females look different to the males,** like this Common Blue (see right and page 11). Make sure you study the pictures and the text carefully. The male (♂) and female (♀) wings are shown for each species.

6 **What month is it?** Many butterflies are seen only at certain times of the year. See the fact caption for each butterfly.

7 **If you still can't find the butterfly,** you may have to look in a larger field guide (see page 78 for some suggestions). You may have seen a very rare butterfly! Or it might be a moth (see page 59).

Habitat Picture Bands

This book is divided into different habitats (or types of countryside). Each habitat has a different picture band at the top of the page. These are shown below.

Farms, Parks & Gardens

Bogs & Marshes

Heath, Scrub & Valleys

Meadows

Mountains

Woodlands

When the adult inside the chrysalis is fully formed, the chrysalis splits and a wet butterfly crawls out. The butterfly inflates its wings, lets them dry, and then flies off in search of nectar.

What To Look For

Parts of a butterfly

Like all insects, a typical adult butterfly has three parts to its body, and three pairs of legs. The three body parts are the head, the thorax, and the abdomen.

Each butterfly has two pairs of wings: two forewings and two hindwings. The wings are covered in scales, which give them their colour. When trying to identify a butterfly, check the following:

- Is it large or small?
- What colour and shape are its wings?
- Do they have patterns on them?
- Don't forget to look under the wings, as the colour and patterns there may be completely different.
- What are the antennae like?

The head has a pair of antennae, which are club-shaped at the tip, and a pair of big eyes, called compound eyes.

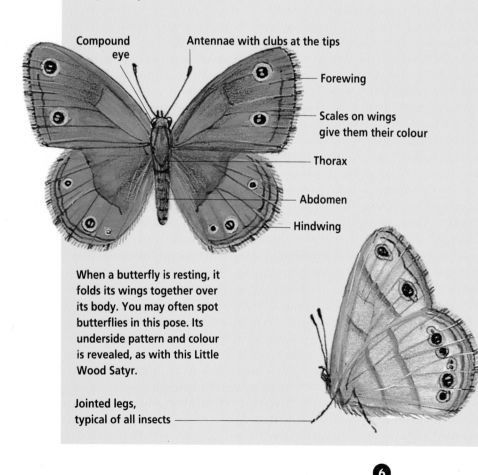

Compound eye

Antennae with clubs at the tips

Forewing

Scales on wings give them their colour

Thorax

Abdomen

Hindwing

When a butterfly is resting, it folds its wings together over its body. You may often spot butterflies in this pose. Its underside pattern and colour is revealed, as with this Little Wood Satyr.

Jointed legs, typical of all insects

Wing shapes

The wing shapes of butterflies vary from rounded to triangular, to long and thin. Some wings have 'tails' on them; others have wavy edges.

The Holly Blue's hindwings are rounded and fringed (page 11)

The Two-tailed Pasha (page 74) has two tails on its hindwings

The Comma's hindwings have wavy edges (page 14)

The Small Skipper's wings are triangular in shape (page 16)

Antennae

Looking at a butterfly's antennae is a useful way to identify them as they vary from type to type.

All Skippers have antennae that hook outwards

The Small Apollo's antennae are stripy

Families of Butterflies

Colour & markings

The colour and markings (or patterns) on a butterfly's wings are one of the first things that you'll notice about it.

The Swallowtail (page 54) has orange and black marks on its hindwings called 'eyespots.' These look like big eyes and frighten away would-be predators.

Male butterflies often have a black mark near the top of the forewing, like the one on this Large Skipper (page 19).

The Silver-washed Fritillary (page 17) has a very noticeable pattern of black dots, dashes, and crescents on orange.

Swallowtails, Apollos & Festoons

These butterflies are quite large, and lively fliers. The 'true' Swallowtails (see left) are all brightly coloured and have tails on their hindwings.

Apollos (see page 61) and Festoons are smaller and have no tails.

Whites & Sulphurs

Butterflies in this group are medium-sized, and are often white or yellow. Some of them have bright orange tips to their wings. Males and females often look quite different, as do these Great Sooty Satyrs (see page 63).

Skippers

These are the smallest of all butterflies, and also the most numerous in Europe. The name 'Skipper' comes from the way that they fly – with a rapid, skipping movement. Like this Grizzled Skipper (see page 45), they have very distinctive hooked antennae, and also quite hairy bodies, and triangular wings.

Brush Footed Butterflies

This is a very large group of butterflies. They are often medium-sized. The feature that really ties them together is the fact that they don't have six 'working' legs like other butterflies. Their forelegs are small and are no use for walking. They are usually fast fliers.

They include the Browns and Ringlets (Satyridae), which are usually some shade of brown; the Fritillaries; the 'aristocrats' – Emperors, Admirals, Pashas, etc.; and the Snouts and Monarchs.

Blues, Coppers, Hairstreaks & Metalmarks

These butterflies are usually small and colourful, and like wild flowers. Blues, like this Large Blue (see page 10), are usually blue; while the Coppers are usually copper-coloured.

The Hairstreaks usually have small tails and a fine line crossing the underside of the hindwing.

Metalmarks, like this Duke of Burgundy Fritillary (page 52), get their name from the shiny, metallic markings on their wings that glint in the sunshine.

Farms, Parks & Gardens

Some butterflies feed at very common plants like nettles, and these are the ones that you are most likely to see without too much hunting. You may well see the butterflies from this section in the other habitats covered in this book – meadows, mountains, woodlands, bogs and wetlands. However, butterflies from those sections may also live in other types of landscape.

Roads in the country and the edges of fields are good places to spot butterflies, as there are often wild flowers growing there for them to visit. So next time you go for a drive in the country, or even along a motorway, keep a lookout for butterflies on the grassy edges.

Parks and gardens are ideal places to spot butterflies. They are filled with colourful flowers just perfect for sipping nectar from, and leaves just waiting to be nibbled by hungry caterpillars. A more unlikely habitat is waste ground, but it often gives a home to lots of butterflies. Waste ground includes railway yards and vacant plots of land which often have fast-growing weeds and hardy wild flowers growing through cracks in the concrete. The butterflies feed on very familiar weeds, such as buddleia, docks and daisies. This picture shows eight species from this section; how many can you recognize?

Red Admiral, Common Blue, Wall Brown, Comma, Silver-washed Fritillary, Peacock, Large Chequered Skipper, Green-veined White.

Marbled White

This butterfly is easy to recognize with its striking black and white colouring. The top of the wings have a black background with white spots. Their undersides have a similar pattern, but are not so brightly marked and have a yellowish tinge. You'll find the Marbled White flying in the summer, in open grassy areas, sipping nectar from flowers. The caterpillars are green, which camouflages them well against the grasses on which they feed.

Species: *Melanargia galathea*
Family: Satyridae
Size: Up to 54 mm
Flight period: One; flies in June and July
Distribution: Western Europe

Grayling

This large butterfly has light brown wings, with light orange areas. There are two eyespots on the forewings, and one on each hindwing. Underneath, the wings have a complex pattern which gives excellent camouflage against the ground and also the bark of trees. There are also eyespots on the undersides, which makes it even more difficult for predators to catch them. Graylings live in grassy areas and near coastal cliffs, and drink sap from trees. Caterpillars feed on different types of grasses.

Species: *Hipparchia semele*
Family: Satyridae
Size: Up to 50 mm
Flight period: One; flies between May and August
Distribution: Most of Europe; not in northern Scandinavia

Large Blue

Species: *Maculinea arion*
Family: Lycaenidae
Size: Up to 40 mm
Flight period: One; flies in June and July
Distribution: Western and central Europe

This butterfly has bright blue wings with black spots on the upper forewing. Females have larger black spots than males. A dark band outlines the wings, enclosed by a white fringe. Underneath, the wings are light brown with dark spots and a bluish tinge at the base of the hindwings. The Large Blue can be seen in flowery meadows. At first, their caterpillars feed on thyme plants, and then they are carried off by ants into their nests. Here, the ants suck a milky liquid from the caterpillars, while the caterpillars feed on the ant grubs.

Holly Blue

This little butterfly has rounded wings, which are lilac blue. Females look different because they have broad black borders on their wings. Underneath, both males and females are a delicate blue colour, with little black spots. The Holly Blue can be seen fluttering around bushes and trees in waysides, clearings and gardens. Holly Blue caterpillars are unusual because they feed on different plants at different times of the year: holly in the spring, and ivy in the autumn.

Species: *Celastrina argiolus*
Family: Lycaenidae
Size: Up to 32 mm
Flight period: Two; flies in April/May and June/July
Distribution: Most of Europe except northern Scandinavia

Long-tailed Blue

So-called because of the long 'tails' on its wings, males of this butterfly are a bright violet colour. Females are less bright and have brown hindwings. Eyespots on the base of the hindwings confuse hungry predators. The undersides of the wings are mottled with wavy lines. The Long-tailed Blue flies in flowery meadows. Its caterpillars feed on plants in the pea family, and sometimes eat each other.

Species: *Lampides boeticus*
Family: Lycaenidae
Size: Up to 36 mm
Flight period: Three; flies between May and September
Distribution: Southern Europe, migrates occasionally to Britain

Common Blue

Male and female Common Blues hardly look like the same butterfly at all. The males have bright blue wings that glint in the sun, while females usually have brown wings with a row of orange spots around the margins. Both males and females have white outlines around their wings, and the undersides are light brown and speckled. The Common Blue, as its name suggests, can be easily spotted, especially in flowery meadows and open grassy areas. Caterpillars feed on vetches and clover.

Species: *Polyommatus icarus*
Family: Lycaenidae – Size: Up to 36 mm
Flight period: Three; flies between April and September
Distribution: Southern and northern Europe

Lang's Short-tailed Blue

Males of this butterfly have violet wings, while females have grey-brown wings. There is a little tail on the end of each hindwing, as well as two spots. Underneath, the wings are mottled brown and cream. Look for this butterfly flying in flowery areas. Caterpillars feed on plants in the pea family.

Species: *Syntaracus pirithous*
Family: Lycaenidae
Size: Up to 26 mm
Flight period: Two; flies between March and July
Distribution: Southern Europe

Little Blue

♂♀ ♂

This is indeed a little butterfly, and is often called the 'Small Blue'. Both males and females have dark brown wings, and males have a blue tinge on their wings. The undersides of the wings are pale, with black spots and blue bases. Caterpillars, which are yellow, feed on kidney vetch flowers. Look for the Little Blue flitting from flower to flower in grassy areas and on cliffs by the coast.

Species: *Cupido minimus*
Family: Lycaenidae – Size: Up to 24 mm
Flight period: Two; flies between April and September
Distribution: Most of Europe, except the extreme north and south

Ringlet

This butterfly gets its name from the string of ringed eyespots along the undersides of the wings. On top, the ringlet is a dark brown, with two spots on each fore- and hindwing. You can tell the females by their slightly paler colour. Look for the Ringlet in wet grassy places, such as ditches or woodland glades. Caterpillars feed on grass during the night.

♂♀

♂

Species: *Aphantopus hyperantus*
Family: Satyridae
Size: Up to 48 mm
Flight period: One; flies between June and August
Distribution: Central Europe eastwards, not Italy nor most of Spain, nor northern Finland, Sweden and Norway

Oberthur's Grizzled Skipper

This little butterfly has soft brown wings with lighter markings. Underneath, the hindwings are reddish brown and covered in vivid light marks. The forewing undersides are black with a definite spot on each wing. Look for this butterfly on flowery slopes.

♂♀ ♂

Species: *Pyrgus armoricanus*
Family: Hesperiidae – Size: Up to 28 mm
Flight period: Two; flies between May and September
Distribution: Central Europe

Large Chequered Skipper

This butterfly may look dull above, with its plain brown colouring, but a flash of its undersides reveals a garish pattern of big white spots on a yellow background. The upper forewings have some tiny marks, and females have chequered black and white fringes around their wings. This butterfly lives in waysides and meadows, and can be seen in the summer. Its caterpillars feed on grasses.

Species: *Heteropterus morpheus*
Family: Hesperiidae
Size: Up to 38 mm
Flight period: One; flies between June and July
Distribution: Spain, central and southern Europe to Iran

♂♀ ♂

Meadow Brown

Females of this butterfly boast a more colourful pattern and a larger size. They are brown with a big orange patch on each forewing, as well as a large eyespot. Males are all brown, with only a hint of orange on the forewings, and much smaller eyespots. Underneath, the wings are paler in colour, with a light band. As the name suggests, you can see this butterfly flying in grassy meadows or roadsides in the summer. Its caterpillars are green and yellow and feed on grasses.

Species: *Maniola jurtina*
Family: Satyridae – **Size:** Up to 50 mm
Flight period: Two; two to three generations per year; flies between June and September
Distribution: Most of Europe, not Finland, Sweden and Norway

Dusky Meadow Brown

Males of this butterfly are mostly brown, and have one or two eyespots on the forewings, as well as a dark streak. Females are larger, with two clearer spots on the forewings, as well as on the underside. Both males and females have dark hindwings, above and below. The Dusky Meadow Brown flies in grassy areas in the summer, and its caterpillars feed on meadow grasses.

Species: *Hyponophele lycaon*
Family: Satyridae
Size: Up to 48 mm
Flight period: One; flies between June and August
Distribution: Central and southern England

Large Wall Brown

This butterfly lives up to its name in every way: it is large, brown and often sits on walls, basking in the sun. The wings have a brown background, with orange and black markings, a large eyespot on each forewing, and two on each hindwing. Females have more orange markings than males. Underneath, the wings are patterned in silvery-grey, with a ring of eyespots on each hindwing. When not sunbathing on walls and rocks, this butterfly can be seen flying in grassy areas. Caterpillars feed on different types of grasses.

Species: *Lasiommata maera*
Family: Satyridae
Size: Up to 56 mm
Flight period: Two; flies between June and September
Distribution: Most of Europe

Red Admiral

♂♀

This handsome, large butterfly is hard to miss. It has bright red bars crossing its forewings, which are black at the top, and spotted with white. The hindwings have orange bars on their borders. Underneath, the wings have a mottled pattern of black, brown and blue. The Red Admiral flies around flowery areas, hedgerows, woodland clearings and gardens. It likes to drink water from puddles and sap from trees, and will also drink juice from rotting fruit in the autumn. Caterpillars feed on nettle leaves.

Species: *Vanessa atalanta*
Family: Nymphalidae – Size: Up to 64 mm
Flight period: One; flies between May and October
Distribution: Western Europe

♂

Peacock

The trademarks of this beautiful butterfly are the four big eyespots on its wings. They are set against a rich red-brown background, and there are also shades of blue, black, white and yellow. A dark margin surrounds the wings, and underneath, they are almost black. Sunshine lovers, Peacocks sip nectar and sunbathe along waysides, in glades and in gardens. If threatened by predators, they flash their coloured eyespots. Caterpillars are black and hairy, and feed on nettle leaves.

Species: *Inachis io* – Family: Nymphalidae – Size: Up to 60 mm
Flight period: One; flies between March and September
Distribution: Most of Europe; not the extreme north and south

♂♀

♂

Comma

♂♀

♂

With its ragged outline, the Comma is well camouflaged against leaves and tree bark. Its wings are patterned with orange and brown on top, and brown underneath, with the white 'comma' mark that gives it its name on the hindwing. Comma caterpillars look like bird droppings to avoid being eaten by predators. They feed on hop leaves and nettles. Look for the Comma on sunny days, sipping nectar from flowers in gardens, on farmland and on roadsides.

Species: *Polygonia c-album*
Family: Nymphalidae – Size: Up to 48 mm
Flight period: Two; flies between March and July
Distribution: Most of Europe

Gatekeeper

You will find this orange-brown butterfly around country hedgerows in the summer . Males are smaller than females, and have a deeper orange colour. They also have a dark streak along the forewings. Both males and females have eyespots on the forewings to confuse predators. Gatekeepers sip nectar from marjoram, wood sage, valerian and bramble flowers. Their caterpillars feed on various types of grasses.

Species: *Pyronia tithonus*
Family: Satyriidae – **Size:** Up to 38 mm
Flight period: One; flies between July and August
Distribution: Central and southern Europe

Chestnut Heath

This butterfly's name comes from the chestnut colour of its forewings, which is much lighter in the females. The forewings are chestnut underneath, too. The hindwings are brown and have a row of dark eyespots underneath. The Chestnut Heath flies in grassy areas in the summer. Caterpillars feed on grasses.

Species: *Coenonympha glycerion*
Family: Satyriidae – **Size:** Up to 36 mm
Flight period: One; flies between June and July
Distribution: Northern Spain, central/southern France, from the Alps eastwards

Dark Green Fritillary

This butterfly gets its name not from its upper colour, but from the colour underneath its hindwing. On top, it is orange-brown with black markings. The underside colour is the best way to identify this butterfly. Look for the silvery spots on the green background. The Dark Green Fritillary flits quickly between flowers in glades,and on waysides and heaths. Caterpillars feed on violet leaves.

Species: *Argynnis aglaja*
Family: Nymphalidae – **Size:** Up to 58 mm
Flight period: One; flies between June and August
Distribution: Most of Europe

Pallas's Fritillary

This butterfly's tiger-like colouring and markings make it easy to spot. Its wings are bright orange with black marks. Underneath, the hindwings are greenish on the inside and reddish on the outside. Pallas's Fritillary can be seen flying along flowery waysides and in glades in the summer. Its caterpillars feed on bog violets.

Species: *Argyronome laodice*
Family: Nymphalidae
Size: Up to 58 mm
Flight period: One; flies between July and August
Distribution: Central and eastern Europe eastwards

Essex Skipper

This butterfly is so-called because it was first identified in Essex, England. It has orange-brown wings outlined in black, and males have a dark streak on their forewings. Underneath, the wings are dusky brown-green. The best way to identify this butterfly is to look for the black tips on the underside of the antennae. The Essex Skipper flies quickly in grassy areas, meadows and roadsides, where its caterpillars can feed on blades of grass.

Species: *Thymelicus lineola*
Family: Hesperiidae – Size: Up to 28 mm
Flight period: One; flies between May and August
Distribution: Central and southern Europe

Small Skipper

You might think at first glance that this was an Essex Skipper, but look again. The Small Skipper does not have black tips on the underside of its antennae. Apart from this, the two are almost exactly the same. The wings are orange-brown with a black outline. Underneath they are paler. Males have a dark streak on their forewings, longer than that of the Essex Skipper. The small skipper can be seen in the summer, flying swiftly through grassy meadows, sipping the nectar of wild flowers. Its caterpillars feed on grass.

Species: *Thymelicus sylvestris*
Family: Hesperiidae
Size: Up to 32 mm
Flight period: One; flies between June and August
Distribution: Northern Europe to Iran

Marbled Fritillary

This butterfly's rounded wings are orange, speckled with black marks. The undersides of the hindwings are yellowish towards the body, fading to purplish on the outer edge. Females are bigger than males. The Marbled Fritillary flies in flowery waysides, on both lowland and upland. Its caterpillars feed on bramble.

Species: *Brenthis daphne*
Family: Nymphalidae
Size: Up to 54 mm
Flight period:
One; flies between June and August
Distribution:
Southwestern Europe

Lesser Fiery Copper

This butterfly is so-called because of the fiery orange colour to the wings. Males have orange forewings, and paler hindwings with a row of black marks. Females are slightly different, with forewings and hindwings covered in black marks. Underneath, the hindwings are white-grey and speckled with black spots and an orange band around the edge. The Lesser Fiery Copper likes scrub and waste ground and light woodlands. Its caterpillars feed on docks and broom.

Species: *Thersamonia thersamon*
Family: Lycaenidae – Size: Up to 32 mm
Flight period: Two; flies between April and August
Distribution: Italy and eastern Europe

Silver-washed Fritillary

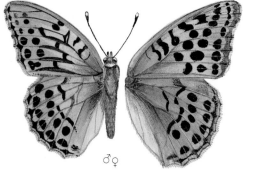

♂♀

This is a big, colourful butterfly that is easy to recognize. Its wings are golden-orange with black spots. Males can be identified by the black stripes on their forewings. Underneath the hindwings you can see the reason for the name of this butterfly: there is a silvery 'wash' over a greenish background colour. Look for the Silver-washed Fritillary in sunny, flowery clearings in woodlands, in farmland areas and on flowery waysides. Its caterpillars feed on violet leaves.

Species: *Argynnis paphia*
Family: Nymphalidae – **Size:** Up to 70 mm
Flight period: One; flies between June and August
Distribution: Most of Europe except the extreme north and south

Large Tortoiseshell

This large butterfly has scalloped edges to its wings, which are orange, patterned with black blotches and a row of blue half-moon shapes outlining the hairy hindwings. The undersides of the wings are dark. The Large Tortoiseshell flies along country lanes and on the edges of woodlands. You'll need to look up to see one, as they like to fly high in the treetops. Their caterpillars feed on the leaves of elm, poplar and willow trees.

Species: *Nymphalis polychloros*
Family: Nymphalidae – **Size:** Up to 64 mm
Flight period: One; flies between June and October
Distribution: Central and southern Europe

♂♀

♂

Small Tortoiseshell

♂♀

♂

Small Tortoiseshells are smaller than Large Tortoiseshells, and have much brighter colouring. However the colouring is similar: orange and black, with a row of blue half-moon shapes that run around both fore- and hindwings. There is also a white mark at the tip of each forewing. Underneath, the hindwings are dark. These butterflies flutter around flowers in gardens, farmland and waysides. They are also frequently seen as migrants on high mountains. Caterpillars are black and yellow, and covered in black spines. They feed on nettle leaves.

Species: *Aglais urticae* – **Family:** Nymphalidae
Size: Up to 50 mm
Flight period: Two; flies between May and October
Distribution: Most of Europe, not northern Scandinavia

Small Heath

Species: *Coenonympha*
Family: Satyridae
Size: Up to 32 mm
Flight period: Three; flies between May and September
Distribution: Most of Europe, not northern Scandinavia

This little butterfly has light brown to orange wings with darker margins and a single spot on each forewing. The underside of the forewing also has a spot, and that of the hindwing is darker with a row of faint circles running along the edge. Females are larger than males. The Small Heath lives in grassy areas, from meadows to moorland, and along roadside verges and ditches. Look for it resting on grass with its wings closed. The caterpillars feed on grasses.

Provençal Fritillary

So called because it can be found in Provence, France, this butterfly is very brightly patterned with wavy lines crossing orange and yellow stripes. There is a thick black band near the edge of each forewing. Underneath, the hindwing has a row of orange spots. Look for the Provençal Fritillary in flowery waysides and pastures. Caterpillars feed on toadflax.

Species: *Mellicta deione*
Family: Nymphalidae
Size: Up to 46 mm
Flight period: Two; flies between May and September
Distribution: Southwestern Europe

Wall Brown

Also known as the Wall, this butterfly is brightly patterned with black and brown markings against an orange background. There is an eyespot on each forewing, and males also have a strong black streak on their forewings. The underside of the hindwings has a row of eyespots against a mottled silver-grey background. As well as sunbathing on walls and rocks, the Wall Brown likes to fly by waysides and hedgerows, visiting flowers for nectar. Caterpillars feed on many types of grasses.

Species: *Lasiommata megera*
Family: Satyridae
Size: Up to 50 mm
Flight period: Three; flies between March and September
Distribution: Europe except northern Finland, Sweden and Norway

Lulworth Skipper

So-called because it was first identified in Lulworth Cove, Dorset, this butterfly is olive brown. Males have a curved streak on their forewings, and females have a broken circle of pale brown on theirs. The undersides of both males and females are pale brown. The Lulworth Skipper likes grassy slopes on coastal cliffs. It sips nectar from wild flowers such as cow parsley and marjoram. Caterpillars feed on grass.

♂♀   ♀

Species: *Thymelicus acteon*
Family: Hesperiidae
Size: Up to 26 mm
Flight period: One; flies between May and July
Distribution: Central and southern Europe to Iran

Silver-spotted Skipper

♂♀   ♂

Species: *Hesperia comma*
Family: Hesperiidae
Size: Up to 35 mm
Flight period: One; flies between July and August
Distribution: Central, northern and southern Europe to Iran

This skipper is so called because of the silver spots on the green underside of its hindwings. On top, the wings are brown with orange markings. Males can be distinguished by the dark streak on their forewings. The Silver-spotted Skipper lives in grassy areas and meadows on chalky soils, where it feeds on flowers. Caterpillars, which are green with a black head, feed on types of grasses.

Large Skipper

The Large Skipper is dark with orange markings. Males have a strong dark streak on their forewings. Underneath, the wings are greenish with faint orange marks. This butterfly lives in grassy areas such as meadows, coastal cliffs and woodland clearings. Here, it likes to bask in the sun with its wings raised. The caterpillars feed on grasses.

♂♀

♂

Species: *Ochlodea venata*
Family: Hesperiidae
Size: Up to 35 mm
Flight period:
Three; flies between July and August
Distribution:
Most of Europe, except extreme north

Small White

Like the Large White only smaller, Small White males also have one black spot on their forewings. Small Whites can be found everywhere, especially in urban areas. Their caterpillars feed on cabbage plants, but are difficult to detect, because they start eating the heart of the cabbage, where they are well hidden. Unlike Large White caterpillars, Small White caterpillars are green, so they are well camouflaged against the green leaves.

Species: *Pieris rapae*
Family: Pieridae
Size: Up to 54 mm
Flight period:
Three; flies between March and September
Distribution: Throughout Europe

Southern Small White

This butterfly is similar to the Small White, but it only lives in southern areas of Europe. It has white wings with black forewing tips, and black spots which merge with the edge via black veins. Underneath, the wings are yellowish with black speckles. The small white flies in farmland and urban areas. Its caterpillars feed on wild crucifers.

Species: *Pieris mannii*
Family: Pieridae – Size: Up to 46 mm
Flight period: Four; flies between March and September
Distribution: Southern Europe and the Alps

Small Copper

This butterfly has coppery forewings with a black margin and black spots, while the hindwings are almost the reverse, dark with a copper margin. Sometimes there is a row of blue spots along the hindwings as well. Females are larger and have more rounded wings. The undersides are pale brown with black spots. Small Coppers are easy to spot in gardens, on railway embankments and in meadows. They often bask in the sun with their wings open. Caterpillars feed on sorrel and dock leaves.

Species: *Lycaena phlaeus*
Family: Lycaenidae
Size: Up to 30 mm
Flight period: Two; flies between February and August
Distribution: Most of Europe

Green-veined White

As the name suggests, this butterfly is like the Small White, but the veins on its underside are outlined with streaks of green. Above, the wings are whitish, with grey scales and a yellowy tinge. Females have darker markings, and an extra black spot on the forewing. The Green-veined White flies in gardens, damp meadows and ditches, as well as waysides and woodland edges. Its caterpillars only feed on wild members of the cabbage family, so are not pests to cabbage growers.

Species: *Pieris napi*
Family: Pieridae
Size: Up to 48mm
Flight period: Three; flies between April and September
Distribution: Throughout Europe

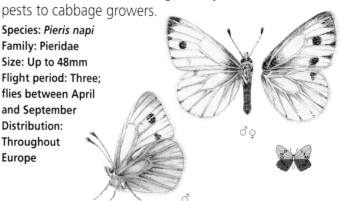

Monarch

This is a butterfly which is hard to miss, partly because of its great size, and also because of its bright orange colour and black patterns. It has black veins crossing its wings, and a black border sprinkled with white spots. The Monarch is an American butterfly, but it can travel the huge distance to visit Europe in the autumn. It flutters around flowery waysides, feeding on buddleia and Michaelmas daisies. The caterpillars of the Monarch are off-white with black and yellow stripes. Their foodplant gives the Monarch its other name, the 'Milkweed'. Eating milkweed makes the caterpillars poisonous if eaten.

Species: *Danaus plexippus*
Family: Danaidae
Size: Up to 100 mm
Flight period: Mostly autumn as immigrant from America
Distribution: Western Europe

Cardinal

This large butterfly is greenish with dark markings. Females are larger than males, and have bolder markings. Underneath, the hindwings are green and the forewings have a red-orange flush at the base. It flies along waysides, in meadows and glades. The caterpillars eat violets.

Species:
Pandoriana pandora
Family: Nymphalidae – Size: Up to 80 mm
Flight period: One; flies between June and July
Distribution: Southern Europe eastwards

Large White

This butterfly has big white wings with black tips on the forewings. Females also have two black spots and a dash on their forewings. The undersides of the wings are yellowish. Large Whites can be found in most habitats, especially urban areas. They, and Small Whites, are popularly known as 'Cabbage Whites', because their brightly coloured caterpillars feed on the outer leaves of cabbage plants, where they are easily spotted. However, birds know not to attack them, as they are poisonous.

Species: *Pieris brassicae*
Family: Pieridae
Size: Up to 64 mm

Flight period: Three; flies between April and October
Distribution:
Throughout Europe

A Butterfly Safari

Wherever you go butterfly-watching, there are a few items which will be valuable to you. The main things that you need are this guide book and your field notebook.

Essential equipment

When you go looking for insects, it is a good idea to take these pieces of equipment with you:

1. **Hand lens:** helps you to look at a basking butterfly or a caterpillar on a leaf close up and in great detail. Buy a folding one that magnifies things 4 or 6 times (labelled x4 or x6) and wear it on a cord around your neck.
2. **Glass or plastic jars** with holes bored in the lid: useful if you find a large caterpillar and want to put it somewhere safe while you look at it.
3. **A little paintbrush:** useful if you want to lift up a caterpillar for a closer look.
4. **Aerial net:** for trapping butterflies and moths temporarily (see opposite).
5. **Beating tray, sheet, or pale umbrella:** for investigating trees and bushes (see page 35).
6. **Camera:** you can take a quick snapshot of the habitat and the plant on which you have found it.
7. **Binoculars:** useful if you want to watch butterflies at a distance or in flight.
8. **Pair of gloves:** some caterpillars can give you a nasty rash from their prickly hairs.
9. **Field notebook and pens:** always take notes of the weather, the date, where you go, and what you find.
10. **Box of coloured pencils:** for field sketches of butterflies.
11. **Lightweight backpack:** this is the most comfortable way to carry your equipment and leaves your hands free.

Field sketches

When you see a butterfly you don't recognize, make a quick sketch in your field notebook. If you start looking it up in your guide book, it will have flown away by the time you find it! Draw its outline first, then fill in more important details, using your coloured pencils. Points to look for are:

- What size was the butterfly? Record a quick estimation of its wingspan.
- Was it one plain colour? Note it down.
- Was the butterfly patterned? What colours and shapes were the different patterns?
- Could you see what its antennae were like?
- What kind of flower was it feeding from?
- Did it fly in a particular way (see page 7)?

Also, make a note of the habitat you were in when you spotted the butterfly. This will make it easier for you to look it up in your field guide later.

Turn the mouth of the net downward to stop the butterfly escaping.

Press the net gently against the ring to trap the butterfly at the bottom.

Using an aerial net

It is best to buy a lightweight aerial net from a company that specializes in supplying insect-collecting equipment. The net itself should be made of lightweight nylon or muslin. The trick is to turn the mouth of the net sideways, once the butterfly is inside. Then the mouth of the net will be covered by material and the butterfly cannot escape.

Hold a butterfly only by its folded wings, very gently between your thumb and forefinger.

Bogs & Marshes

These damp, watery areas also include such freshwater habitats as pond and river banks, swamps, and peat bogs. The water can be fresh or salt. You may also find boggy areas in the middle of forests and on mountainsides.

Around wetland areas, you may see large groups of butterflies gathered around muddy puddles, drinking the water. This is called mud-puddling, and provides the butterflies with special minerals. It is a common sight in warmer climates, and is an ideal moment to observe them.

Butterflies that live in wetland habitats are particularly at risk from pollution from houses, cars and factories. When looking around wetlands, tread very carefully – you may sink into the mushy ground. This picture shows five species from this section; how many can you recognize?

Large Copper, Frigga's Fritillary, Marsh Fritillary, Baltic Grayling, Moorland Clouded Yellow.

Red Underwing Skipper

This little butterfly gets its name from the reddish tinge to the underside of its hindwings, which also have white marks. Above, the wings are brown, and dotted with rows of white spots. The Red Underwing Skipper lives in tundra, bogs and moors. Look out for it during the summer, flying near great burnet, raspberry and cinquefoil, which its caterpillars feed on.

Species: *Spialia sertorius*
Family: Hesperiidae
Size: Up to 26 mm
Flight period: One; flies between June and July
Distribution: Central and southern Europe

Cranberry Fritillary

This butterfly's wings are orange with dark dots and dashes. The hindwings have a darker base than the forewings. Underneath, the hindwings have rich brown-red, silver and yellow marks, while the forewings have black marks. You can tell the females apart because they are larger and darker than the males. The Cranberry Fritillary flies in bogs, marshes and on wet heaths in the summer months.

Species: *Boloria aquilonaris*
Family: Nymphalidae
Size: Up to 34 mm
Flight period: One; flies between June and August
Distribution: Central Europe

Baltic Grayling

Females of this butterfly are much larger than males, and have rounded forewings. Both males and females are brown, with a row of yellowish blotches running down their wings. There are black spots within some of the blotches, and these are larger in the females. Underneath, the hindwings are mottled grey. The Baltic Grayling flies in boggy areas near pine woods. The caterpillars are striped pale green with reddish hairs; they eat sedges, rushes or grasses.

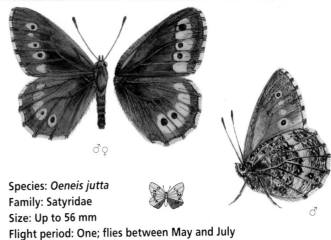

Species: *Oeneis jutta*
Family: Satyridae
Size: Up to 56 mm
Flight period: One; flies between May and July
Distribution: Baltic States, Finland, Sweden, Norway and northern Russia

Freija's Fritillary

This butterfly can be found in Europe. It is tawny orange with a busy pattern of dark spots and bands. Underneath, the hindwing is reddish brown, with white bars near the margin and zigzag marks in the middle. You'll find Freija's Fritillary in forest clearings, on heaths and moors and in tundra.

Species: *Clossiana freija*
Family: Nymphalidae – Size: Up to 44 mm
Flight period: One; flies between May and June
Distribution: Scandinavia and the Baltic States

Frigga's Fritillary

You can find this butterfly in North America as well as Europe. It is orange on top, with dark bars and spots. The undersides are patterned in a similar way but have white marks on the margin, a reddish tinge and a yellowish row of marks running along them. Frigga's Fritillary flies in bogs and moors and likes to bask on sunny days with its wings spread out. The caterpillars feed on cloudberry.

Species: *Clossiana frigga*
Family: Nymphalidae – Size: Up to 46 mm
Flight period: One; flies between June and July
Distribution: Finland, Sweden and Norway

Marsh Fritillary

The vivid patterns on this butterfly's wings make it easy to spot. Against a dark background, there are blotches, dots and dashes in orange, yellow and black. The undersides repeat the pattern, but the colours are lighter. The Marsh Fritillary is so-called because it lives in moist places such as marshes, bogs and wet waysides. It was once called the "Greasy Fritillary" because of the greasy or shiny look to the forewing undersides. The black caterpillars feed on devil's-bit scabious, as well as foxglove, wood sage and honeysuckle.

Species: *Eurodyas aurinia*
Family: Nymphalidae
Size: Females up to 46 mm; males about 38 - 40 mm
Flight period: One; flies between April and June
Distribution: Western, central, southern and southeastern Europe, Russia, Asia Minor to Korea

Cranberry Blue

Male Cranberry Blues have deep violet blue wings, much brighter than the females, which have brown wings with just a tinge of violet. Underneath, the wings are light brown with red spots and blue dusting on the edge of the hindwing. The Cranberry Blue lives in bogs and moors.

♂♀   ♂

Species: *Vacciniina optilete*
Family: Lycaenidae
Size: Up to 22 mm
Flight period: One; July
Distribution: Mostly northern Europe eastwards and on high moorlands in central Europe

Large Copper

♂♀   ♂

Males and females of this butterfly look different on top. The males have plain copper coloured wings with a black dash on the forewing and dark margins. By contrast, females have wings of a darker copper colour, patterned with black marks. They also have a broad black margin on the forewing. Underneath, both males and females have orange forewings speckled with black marks, and white hindwings, with black marks and an orange border. The Large Copper lives in moist areas such as marshes and fens. Its caterpillars feed on large water dock.

Species: *Lycaena dispar* – **Family:** Lycaenidae
Size: Up to 40 mm – **Flight period:** One; in June/July
Distribution: Central and southeastern Europe

Moorland Clouded Yellow

You'll have no problem telling the males from the females in this butterfly. Males have bright yellow wings, with contrasting broad black borders. Females have very pale cream wings with the black border mainly on the forewing tip. Underneath, males have yellow-orange coloured wings, while females wings are greenish yellow. The Moorland Clouded Yellow flies over bogs in the summer, and it is here that its caterpillars' favourite plant, bog whortleberry, occurs.

♂♀

Species: *Colias palaeno*
Family: Pieridae
Size: Up to 48 mm
Flight period: One; flies between June and July
Distribution: Central and eastern Europe, Scandinavia and Russia

Heath, Scrub & Valleys

Heaths are surprisingly varied in their plants and animals, although they do not have the huge variety of flowering plants found in meadows and pastures (see pages 36–57), which attract so many butterflies to lay their eggs there. Like meadows, they are wide open to the weather, but they can also include single trees, gorse thickets, patches of heather moorland, and clumps of bracken.

Scrub land usually can also be described as open woodland. You will find open spaces with grass and wild flowers, along with dense thickets of sloe, buckthorn and other prickly shrubs.

Around the Mediterranean Sea, much of the land has been turned into dry scrub by too much farming. Most of the trees and shrubs that grow here are evergreens with small leathery leaves that can survive the dryness and heat of summer. There is always a risk of a forest fire during the summer.

Sheltered, steep-sided valleys on mountain hillsides have much the same sort of plant and animal life as you find on heaths and in scrub. They also often have boggy patches where streams run down from the melting snows above. This picture shows five species from this section; how many can you recognize?

Southern White Admiral, Brown Argus, Black Hairstreak, Green Hairstreak, Yellow-legged Tortoiseshell.

Brown Argus

Brown wings, with a row of orange half-moons on the margins, are the trademarks of this butterfly. Underneath, the wings are light brown with orange and black spots. You can tell the females by their larger size, and lighter colouring. Brown Arguses live on heathlands and coastal slopes, where they flit from flower to flower in sociable groups. Caterpillars feed on rock rose and storksbill leaves, and are often seen with ants, which drink a milky fluid from a special honeygland and tiny pores on the caterpillar's body.

Species: *Aricia agestis*
Family: Lycaenidae
Size: Up to 28 mm
Flight period: Three; flies between April and August
Distribution: Central and southern Europe

Mountain Argus

Species: *Aricia artaxerxes*
Family: Lycaenidae
Size: Up to 28 mm
Flight period: One; flies between June and July
Distribution: Central and southern Europe

This butterfly is also known as the 'Northern Argus' or 'Scotch Brown Argus', because experts in eighteenth-century Britain could only find it in Edinburgh. It looks quite similar to the Brown Argus, with its brown wings, and the row of orange marks on the borders, although there are not so many on the forewing borders. The main identification feature is a white mark in the middle of each forewing. It lives on moorland, and is solitary, unlike the sociable Brown Argus. Caterpillars feed on rock-rose leaves.

Sloe Hairstreak

This butterfly is so called because its caterpillars feed on sloe leaves. It has dark brown wings, with a faint orange spot at the base of each hindwing. Each hindwing also has a stubby tail. Underneath, the wings are light tan, with orange marks near the tail. There is also a broken white line running along the wings. The Sloe Hairstreak flies over scrubland, where its caterpillars' foodplant grows in abundance.

Species: *Nordmannia acaciae*
Family: Lycaenidae
Size: Up to 32 mm
Flight period: One; flies between June and July
Distribution: Spain, France, Italy eastwards

Green Hairstreak

On top, this butterfly looks rather dull and brown, but underneath is a different story. The wings (which are tailless) are bright green, hence the name. It's likely you'll see the green colour often, as the Green Hairstreak rests with its wings closed and the undersides visible. There is a row of white dots running down the undersides as well. The Green Hairstreak lives in scrubby areas, from open woodland to waysides and moors. Its caterpillars feed on the leaves of a wide variety of plants, including broom, gorse and bramble.

Species: *Callophrys rubi*
Family: Lycaenidae
Size: Up to 30 mm
Flight period: One; flies between March and April
Distribution: Most of Europe

Black Hairstreak

Species: *Strymonidia pruni*
Family: Lycaenidae
Size: Up to 32 mm
Flight period: One; flies between June and July
Distribution: Northern Spain, western Europe eastwards

The Black Hairstreak is brown, not black. The name comes from the black spots on the undersides of its wings. Above, the brown wings of this butterfly have orange markings around the edges, and there is a small tail on each hindwing. The undersides of the wings are lighter brown, and, as well as black spots, have a wide orange band and a broken white line. Black Hairstreaks live in woodland and scrubby areas where sloe thickets grow. In the spring, their caterpillars feed on sloe flowers and buds.

Blue-spot Hairstreak

The name of this butterfly comes from the blue spot at the base of the tail on the underside of the hindwings. Above, males have brown wings, with two orange spots on each hindwing. Females have a lot of orange on their wings, set against a brown background. The undersides are paler brown, and have orange marks and a broken white line. The Blue-spot Hairstreak flies in scrubby areas, where its caterpillars feed on sloe and buckthorn.

Species: *Strymonidia spini*
Family: Lycaenidae
Size: Up to 32 mm
Flight period: One; flies between June and July
Distribution: Southern and central Europe

Yellow-legged Tortoiseshell

This butterfly looks very similar to the Large Tortoiseshell, except that it has yellow legs. The wings are orange, with scalloped, light-coloured margins. There is a row of blue half-moon shapes inside the margin, and black and yellow markings. The black markings are bolder than those of the Large Tortoiseshell. Underneath, the wings are grey-brown and edged with blue. The Yellow-legged Tortoiseshell flies around valley bottoms and lowlands. Its caterpillars feed on willow leaves.

Species: *Nymphalis xanthomelas*
Family: Nymphalidae
Size: Up to 64 mm
Flight period: One; flies between July and September
Distribution: Eastern Europe eastwards

Southern Comma

This butterfly's wings have a jagged edge, and are greatly indented. It is orange with some dark marks and a row of yellow half-moon shapes running down the margins of both wings. There is a little 'Y' mark on the underside of the hindwing. You'll see the Southern Comma on rocky hillsides and in wooded valleys. Here, its caterpillars feed on pellitory-of-the-wall.

Species: *Polygonia egea*
Family: Nymphalidae
Size: Up to 46 mm
Flight period: Two; flies between May and September
Distribution: Central and southeastern Europe

Nettle Tree Butterfly

The best way to identify this butterfly is to look at the outline of the wings. They are jagged, with an obvious hook on each forewing. Another feature you will notice is the long snout on its head, which has given it another name, the 'Beak Butterfly'. The wings have a brown background, with orange blotches, and a white mark at the top of each forewing. The undersides are plain grey-brown. This butterfly lives in valleys and orchards, and not surprisingly, its caterpillars feed on nettle tree leaves.

Species: *Libythea celtis*
Family: Libytheidae
Size: Up to 44 mm
Flight period: One; flies from March to July until hibernation
Distribution: Portugal through central Europe to southern Europe eastwards

Poplar Admiral

Named after its caterpillar's foodplant, this large butterfly has brown wings with a white band around the upper hindwings, orange semi-circles around the edges and random white marks on the forewings. Females are bigger than males, and have bolder markings. As well as woodland clearings, this butterfly can be found in valleys and woodland rides.

Species: *Ladoga populi*
Family: Nymphalidae – **Size:** Up to 80 mm
Flight period: One; flies between June and August
Distribution: Central and southeastern Europe

Southern White Admiral

This butterfly has big, dark coloured wings with a bluish tinge. There are random white spots on the forewings and a regular band of white spots running along the hindwings. There is also a row of black spots on the margin of the hindwings. The underside has a bright, distinctive pattern with orange and white markings. Look for the Southern White Admiral in sunny woodland clearings and at the bottom of valleys. Caterpillars feed on honeysuckle leaves.

Species: *Ladoga reducta*
Family: Nymphalidae
Size: Up to 56 mm
Flight period: Two;
flies between May
and September
Distribution: Central
and southern Europe

Speckled Wood

The speckled brown wings of this butterfly hide it perfectly in the woodland areas where it lives. Each forewing has a black eyespot, and there are three more eyespots along the base of each hindwing. As well as in woodland, you can see the Speckled Wood along roadsides and in valleys. In Mediterranean countries in Europe, the Speckled Wood has a red-orange tinge to its wings. Caterpillars, which are green, feed on various types of grasses.

Species: *Pararge aegeria*
Family: Satyridae
Size: Up to 45 mm
Flight period: Two;
flies between March and
October – **Distribution:**
Western Europe through Asia
Minor (most of Europe), not Finland,
Sweden and Norway

Butterflies To Be

Most butterflies spend far more time as a caterpillar and a chrysalis than they do as a butterfly (see page 4). If you can find them at an earlier stage, you can watch them develop into an adult butterfly.

Beating for caterpillars

A good way to see tree- or shrub-dwelling caterpillars more clearly is to dislodge them from the branches. You can do this with a sharp blow from a long stick on the branch. Try beating several different types of trees – some caterpillars will feed only on one type.

1 **Stretch a white sheet out under a low tree branch** or make a beating tray (see opposite for how to do it). You can also use a pale umbrella turned upside-down.
2 **Find a long stick** and beat the base of the branch quite sharply. Take care not to damage the tree.
3 **Many different insects, including caterpillars, should drop** on to the beating tray.
4 **You may find it easier** if one person holds the beating tray, and the other uses the stick.

Collecting pupae

Looking for pupae (chrysalises) while out on a country walk can be a challenging task. Some may be buried in the ground or in a pile of leaves. Others may be impossible to spot, as they are so well camouflaged (hidden against the background).

Just like caterpillars, chrysalises need to be inconspicuous. Some chrysalises look like leaves or twigs. Some even have ragged edges and holes that add to the effect. Tiny silver or gold spots on a chrysalis mimic drops of rain. Sometimes they imitate bird droppings, which would be sure to keep any predator (hunter) at bay! Other types of chrysalises seem to draw attention to themselves with bright colours. This shows they are poisonous, so a predator would risk its life.

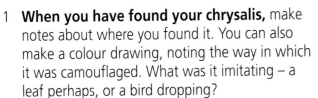

1 **When you have found your chrysalis,** make notes about where you found it. You can also make a colour drawing, noting the way in which it was camouflaged. What was it imitating – a leaf perhaps, or a bird dropping?

2 **Carefully place the pupa in a glass or plastic jar** – in some soil if it was buried.

3 **Take off the lid at home.** Cover the jar with cheesecloth or netting, and put it in the shade.

4 **Check your jars regularly** – every two days or so in the spring.

5 **When it emerges,** take note of what comes out. You may discover that small wasps crawl out. Many types of insects lay their eggs inside the eggs, caterpillars or pupae of butterflies: they are known as parasites.

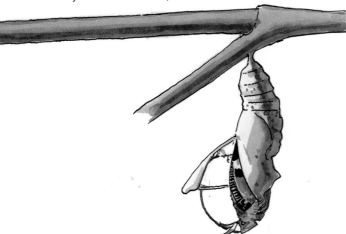

Make a beating tray

An easy way to look at caterpillars that live on trees is to make a beating tray. You will need: two bamboo canes about 45 cm long, one bamboo cane 1 metre long, some white cloth (a piece of old bed sheet will do), strong glue or a stapler, some string or wire, and a long stick.

1 **Place one of the short canes across the top of the long cane** to make a 'T' shape and secure it tightly with some string or wire.

2 **Then lay the other short cane across the middle of the long cane** and fix it with wire or string so that it cannot move around.

3 **Cut enough white cloth to lay across the bamboo frame** and overlap the edges by 5 cm all around.

4 **Lay the cloth on the ground, then lay the frame on top.** Fold the edges of the cloth over the frame and fix it with fabric glue or staples. If this is difficult, ask an adult to help you. If you glue it, don't use the tray until the glue is dry.

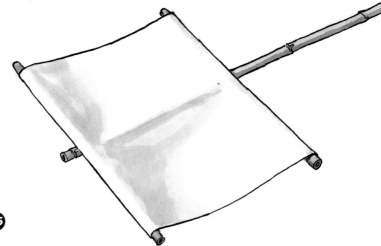

Meadows

Wide, flat, open spaces filled with different types of grasses or flowers are typical of this habitat. They are exposed to wind, rain and sunshine, and get little shelter. Nevertheless, many plants thrive here. Even slow-growing, rare plants can survive here undisturbed if the ground is only used for grazing animals. Meadows and pastures are often teeming with wild flowers, such as sheep sorrel and clovers, which attract butterflies.

Lowland meadows and pastures have long grasses, while downs and limestone uplands have shorter grass. Lowland meadows are cut once a year in early summer for hay (preserved by drying) or silage (preserved by fermentation). Today many meadows and pastures have been ploughed up. Many others have been replanted with newer kinds of cultivated grasses and the flowers have disappeared.

Many butterflies that live in meadows lay their eggs on various grasses, so that their caterpillars can eat them when they hatch. When a meadow is destroyed by over-grazing by farm animals, or by ploughing, a butterfly's favourite plant will disappear. This picture shows eight species from this section;   how many can you recognize?

Adonis Blue, Scarce Copper, Southern Festoon, Queen of Spain Fritillary, Orange Tip, Grizzled Skipper, Safflower Skipper, Clouded Yellow.

Meadows

Amanda's Blue

The males and females of this butterfly are very different indeed. Males are bigger, and have shiny blue wings with dark margins. Females have brown wings, with just a faint scattering of blue scales near the base of the wings. They also have a small row of orange marks along the bottom of the hindwings. Underneath, the wings of both males and females are pale grey with dark spots and orange marks. Females have more distinct markings here. Amanda's Blue lives in flowery meadows, where its caterpillars can feed on tufted vetch.

Species: *Agrodiaetus amanda*
Family: Lycaenidae
Size: Up to 38 mm
Flight period: One; flies between June and July
Distribution: Holland, France, Spain, Sweden, Norway

Meleager's Blue

This large blue has shiny blue wings with brown margins and a scalloped effect at the base of the hindwing, more exaggerated in the females. Underneath, the wings are light brown, and speckled with black and white. Meleager's Blue flies in flowery meadows in the summer. Its caterpillars feed on milk vetch and thyme.

Species: *Meleageria daphnis*
Family: Lycaenidae
Size: Up to 38 mm
Flight period: One; June/July
Distribution: Central and southeastern Europe, not in northern Europe

Silver-studded Blue

The name of this butterfly comes from the row of silver spots on the underside of its hindwing. Above, males and females look quite different. Males are blue, with dark margins, but females are brown, with a row of orange spots. As well as the tell-tale silver spots underneath the wings, there are also black, blue and orange spots set against a pale background. Look out for the Silver-studded Blue flying in flowery meadows and heathland. Caterpillars feed on broom, gorse and rock-rose. Ants like to drink a milky fluid from special glands in their bodies, but this does not harm the caterpillars.

Species: *Plebejus argus*
Family: Lycaenidae
Size: Up to 35 mm
Flight period: Two; flies between May and August
Distribution: Most of Europe except extreme north, south and west

Geranium Blue

♂♀   ♂

No matter how closely you look, you won't find any blue on this butterfly! The males have plain brown wings, while females have brown wings with orange marks on the hindwings. The undersides of the wings are light coloured with black and white markings, a light streak and a band of orange marks along the edge of the hindwing. Flowery mountain meadows are this butterfly's favourite habitat; it breeds on cranesbill.

Species: *Eumedonia eumedon*
Family: Lycaenidae – **Size:** Up to 32 mm
Flight period: Three; flies between April and August
Distribution: Spain, central and southern Europe

Baton Blue

♂♀   ♂

You can recognize this butterfly by the striking chequered margin around its wings. Males have blue wings and females' wings are purple-brown. Underneath the wings look completely different, light grey speckled with black spots, and with a row of orange spots around the margin of the hindwing. Look for the Baton Blue in flowery meadows; it breeds on thyme – attended by ants.

Species: *Pseudophilotes baton*
Family: Lycaenidae
Size: Up to 24 mm
Flight period: Two; flies between April and September
Distribution: Central and southern Europe

Green-undersides Blue

This butterfly gets its confusing name from the blue-green flush on the hindwing underside. There are also noticeable large black spots on the forewing underside. Above, males have blue wings with black margins. Females have brown wings. The Green-undersides Blue flies in flowery meadows, where its caterpillars feed on broom.

♂♀   ♂

Species: *Glaucopsyche alexis*
Family: Lycaenidae – **Size:** Up to 36 mm
Flight period: One; flies between April and June
Distribution: Southern and central Europe

Damon Blue

As with many other blues, the males of this butterfly have blue wings edged in brown, while the females' wings are brown. The best identification to look for is underneath the hindwing. Here, there are black markings and a distinct white streak against a brown background. The Damon Blue flies in flowery meadows, and its caterpillars feed on sainfoin.

♂♀   ♂

Species: *Agrodiaetus damon*
Family: Lycaenidae – **Size:** Up to 32 mm
Flight period: One; flies between July and August
Distribution: Spain, central Europe to southeastern Europe

Meadows

Alcon Blue

Males of this butterfly have blue-violet wings with a dark border and a white fringe on the edges. Females have much darker wings, blue in the middle and sometimes with dark spots on the forewings. The undersides are pale with black markings. The Alcon Blue flies in flowery meadows in the summer. Its caterpillars feed on gentian leaves.

Species: *Maculinea alcon*
Family: Lycaenidae
Size: Up to 38 mm
Flight period: One; flies between June and July
Distribution: Northern Spain and France across Europe

Mazarine Blue

Males of this butterfly have violet-blue wings. Females' wings are brown with a violet tinge at the base. The underside of both males and females is brown with some clear black marks. Look for the Mazarine Blue flying in flowery meadows and heathlands. Caterpillars feed on clovers and kidney vetch.

Species: *Cyanaris semiargus*
Family: Lycaenidae
Size: Up to 35 mm
Flight period: One; flies between July and August
Distribution: Most of Europe except Britain

Chapman's Blue

Males and females of this butterfly hardly look like the same type! Males have blue wings with dark margins edged in white fringes, while females usually have brown wings with orange markings around the edge. The undersides are pale, with orange markings around the margins and black spots. Chapman's Blues fly in flowery meadows. The caterpillars feed on sainfoin leaves.

Species: *Agrodiaetus thersites*
Family: Lycaenidae – **Size:** Up to 32 mm
Flight period: Three; flies between May and September
Distribution: Southern Europe

Idas Blue

This butterfly is similar to Reverdin's Blue, only smaller. The males have violet-blue wings, and females' wings are brown flushed with blue and with some orange marks on the edges. Underneath, males and females have an orange band running around the margin of the wings. The Idas Blue lives in flowery meadows, and its caterpillars feed on members of the pea family. There is a symbiotic relationship with ants when the caterpillars pupate and the adults hibernate inside the ants' nest.

Species: *Lycaeides idas*
Family: Lycaenidae
Size: Up to 30 mm
Flight period: Two; flies between June and August
Distribution: Most of Europe including Finland, Sweden and Norway, but not Britain

Short-tailed Blue

This butterfly is so-called because of the tiny tail at the base of each hindwing. The males have violet-blue wings with dark margins. Females have brown wings, with faint blue colouring near the body. The undersides of both males and females are very pale, with a flush of blue at the base, black spots and orange marks near the tail on the hindwing. Look for the Short-tailed Blue on heathlands and flowery hillsides. Here, their caterpillars feed on birds-foot-trefoil and medick.

Species: *Everes argiades*
Family: Lycaenidae
Size: Up to 30 mm
Flight period: Three; flies between April and July
Distribution: Pyrenees, eastwards through Europe

Provençal Short-tailed Blue

Like the Short-tailed Blue, this butterfly has tiny hindwing tails. The other part of its name comes from the fact that it may be seen in Provence, France, as well as other parts of southern Europe. Males have violet-blue wings with a dark border and a white fringe, and females' wings are brown with a white fringe on the edge. The undersides are pale blue with black spots. The lack of orange spots here sets this butterfly apart from other Short-tailed Blues. It flies in damp flowery meadows and heaths, and its caterpillars feed on crown vetch.

Species: *Everes alcetas*
Family: Lycaenidae – Size: Up to 32 mm
Flight period: Three; flies between April and September
Distribution: Through Spain and southern Europe

Reverdin's Blue

Male Reverdin's Blues have violet-blue wings, while females have brown wings with a row of orange marks around the base of the hindwing. The undersides of the wings of both males and females have a band of orange marks around the margin of the wing. Reverdin's Blue flies in flowery meadows, and it is here that its caterpillars find their food plant, crown vetch.

Species: *Lycaeides argyronomon*
Family: Lycaenidae
Size: Up to 34 mm
Flight period: Two; flies between May and August
Distribution: France eastwards across central Europe

Meadows

Escher's Blue

Males of this butterfly have blue wings with white fringes and females are brown with a row of orange marks around the margins. The undersides of both are pale, with black spots and a row of orange spots around the edge. The black spots are stronger in the female. Escher's Blue flies in lowland flowery meadows, in the summertime. Caterpillars feed mostly on medick.

Species: *Agrodiaetus escheri*
Family: Lycaenidae
Size: Up to 38 mm
Flight period: One; flies between June and July
Distribution: Southern Europe, mainly along the northern Mediterranean coast

Turquoise Blue

The name of this butterfly comes from the turquoise colour of the male wings. Females have brown wings, with orange spots along the edges. The undersides of males and females are pale brown with sharp black spots crossing the forewing and pale orange marks around the hindwing. The Turquoise Blue can be seen in flowery meadows, but only in July. The caterpillars feed on clover and thyme.

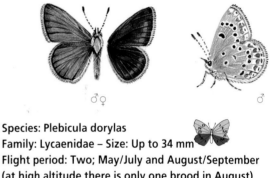

Species: Plebicula dorylas
Family: Lycaenidae – **Size:** Up to 34 mm
Flight period: Two; May/July and August/September
(at high altitude there is only one brood in August)
Distribution: Spain through southern and central Europe

Chalk-hill Blue

Species: *Lysandra coridon*
Family: Lycaenidae
Size: Up to 36 mm
Flight period: One; flies between July and August
Distribution: Throughout Europe

As with many other blues, the males of this butterfly are brightly coloured to attract the females, while the females are dark and drab for camouflage. In this case, the male has silvery-blue wings with dark markings around the edges and black spots on the hindwings, and the female is brown with some orange spots on the hindwing margin. Underneath, the wings are pale in the male, but browner in the female, and speckled with dots and dashes in black, white and orange. As the name suggests, this butterfly likes to fly near chalky hills, as well as in flowery meadows, where it sips nectar from wild flowers. The caterpillars, which are pale green, feed on horseshoe vetch. Ants keep predators away, in return for a drink of milky fluid from special glands in the caterpillar's body.

Osiris Blue

♂♀   ♂

The male of this butterfly has blue-purple wings, which are plain, with no markings. Females look like completely different butterflies, with plain brown wings. The undersides of both are pale with a row of black spots and a blue flush at the base of the wings. The Osiris Blue flies in flowery, mountain meadows in the summer, where its caterpillars feed on sainfoin.

Species: *Cupido osiris*
Family: Lycaenidae
Size: Up to 30 mm
Flight period: Two; flies between May and July
Distribution: North and central Spain, France and eastwards through southern Europe

Dingy Skipper

As its name suggests, this skipper is rather dingy in colour, but it has attractive patterns on its brown wings. There is a delicate grey colour and tiny dark spots on the forewings. The undersides are light brown with white spots. The Dingy Skipper lives in flowery woodland clearings and meadows, and likes to sunbathe with its wings spread out flat. The caterpillars feed on bird's-foot trefoil and crown vetch.

Species: *Erynnis tages*
Family: Hesperiidae
Size: Up to 28mm
Flight period: Two; flies between May and August
Distribution: Most of Europe except extreme northern Europe

♂♀

Violet Copper

This little copper gets its name from the male's colours, a beautiful shiny blue-violet colour. There is a row of orange spots around the edge of its hindwings. Females have an orange-black pattern against a brown background. Underneath, the hindwings are tan with black spots and an orange band inside the margin. The Violet Copper lives in wet meadows. The caterpillars feed on knotgrass.

Species: *Lycaena helle*
Family: Lycaenidae
Size: Up to 28 mm
Flight period: Two; flies between May and October
Distribution: Scattered in central Europe, Finland, Sweden and Norway

♂♀

Adonis Blue

♀♂

♂

Males have beautiful bright blue wings with a fine dark line running around the edge. Females, by contrast, have brown wings, with orange markings on the edges. Both males and females have a chequered white band around all wings, and dark, speckled undersides with orange, black and white markings. The Adonis Blue flies on flowery slopes and in meadows. The caterpillars feed on horseshoe vetch.

Species: *Lysandra bellargus*
Family: Lycaenidae
Size: Up to 36 mm
Flight period: Two; flies between May and September
Distribution: Throughout Europe

Almond-eyed Ringlet

This butterfly is mainly brown, with a row of almond-shaped orange eyespots running inside its wing margins. Females have larger spots with white centres. The underside of the wings is similar to the upperside. Look for the Almond-eyed Ringlet flying high up in alpine meadows, in the summer.

Species: *Erebia alberganus*
Family: Satyridae
Size: Up to 44 mm
Flight period: One; flies in June and July
Distribution: Alps, Apennines, Dolomites

False Heath Fritillary

This dark-coloured butterfly has orange markings, mostly on the forewings. Males are smaller and darker than the females. The underside of the hindwing is much brighter, white, with three yellow bands edged in black crossing the wing. The False Heath Fritillary flies in alpine meadows. The caterpillars feed on cow-wheat and plantain.

Species: *Melitaea diamina*
Family: Nymphalidae – **Size:** Up to 42 mm
Flight period: One, flies between May and July
Distribution: Pyrenees, central and southeastern Europe and Scandinavia

Heath Fritillary

This butterfly has brown wings heavily marked with orange patterns, and a white chequered fringe on the edge. Males have more patterns on their wings than females. Underneath, the wings are brightly patterned, with a yellow margin edged in black, and a striking white bar crossing the hindwing. The Heath Fritillary can be found on heaths, as well as flowery waysides and meadows, where it sips nectar from wild flowers. The caterpillars feed on cow-wheat and plantain.

Species: *Mellicta athalia*
Family: Nymphalidae
Size: Up to 40 mm
Flight period: Two; flies between May and September
Distribution: Throughout most of Europe

Grizzled Skipper

♂♀   ♂

This butterfly has brown and white wings, with grey or 'grizzled' hairs. There is a chequered margin around its wings and the undersides are greenish brown and speckled with white. The Grizzled Skipper lives in flowery meadows and on chalk downs. A fast flier, it enjoys sunny weather, when it sunbathes with its wings spread out flat. The caterpillars feed on wild strawberry cinquefoil, agrimony and mallow.

Species: *Pyrgus malvae*
Family: Hesperiidae
Size: Up to 28 mm
Flight period: Two; flies between April and August
Distribution: Most of Europe

Large Grizzled Skipper

♂♀   ♂

As the name suggests, this butterfly is like the Grizzled Skipper, only slightly larger. The wings are brown, speckled with white spots, which are more pronounced in the male. Underneath, the wings are light olive-green and also speckled in white. The caterpillars' foodplants are cinquefoil, bramble and rock-rose, found in the flowery meadows where this butterfly lives.

Species: *Pyrgus alveus*
Family: Hesperiidae – **Size:** Up to 32 mm
Flight period: Two; flies between June and August
Distribution: Central Europe

Safflower Skipper

♂♀   ♀

This skipper is mostly brown, with uneven white marks on the forewings and dusky orange marks on the hindwings. Underneath, the hindwings have dusky yellow marks, and the forewings have white marks. There is a chequered margin running around the edges of the wings. The Safflower Skipper flies in flowery meadows, where its caterpillars feed on hollyhocks and mallow.

Species: *Pyrgus fritallarius*
Family: Hesperiidae – **Size:** Up to 34 mm

Flight period: One; flies between June and September
Distribution: Central and southern Europe

Mallow Skipper

The attractive wings of this butterfly have a marbled pattern in brown, black and white. The white marks are on the forewings only. The edges of the hindwings are scalloped. Underneath, the wings are pale green, with light bands. The Mallow Skipper lives in flowery places, and its caterpillars feed on mallow, which gives it its name.

Species: *Carcharodus alceae*
Family: Hesperiidae – **Size:** Up to 32 mm

Flight period: Three; flies between April and September
Distribution: Central and southern Europe

♂♀   ♀

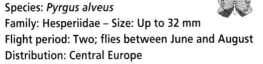

Meadows

Scarce Heath

This butterfly has very dark wings, with a striking row of orange marks around the edge of the hindwings. Underneath, the hindwings are pale brown, with a row of red-orange ringed eyespots, which are a good identification tool. The Scarce Heath flies in damp meadows and moors during May and June. Its caterpillars feed on rye grass, wild iris and sedges.

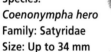

Species:
Coenonympha hero
Family: Satyridae
Size: Up to 34 mm
Flight period: One; flies between May and June
Distribution: Northern France eastwards across central Europe, Scandinavia

Large Heath

This butterfly may confuse you, as it has several different forms, or 'sub-species' which all look a bit different. The wings are generally light brown above with some spots, and dark grey underneath with a row of eyespots. The Large Heath lives in boggy areas and wet meadows, where it likes to rest with its wings folded on grass stems or turf. The caterpillars feed on white beak-sedge, as well as fescues and cottongrass.

Species: *Coenonympha tullia*
Family: Satyridae
Size: Up to 38-40 mm
Flight period: One;
flies between June and July
Distribution: Northern Europe eastwards, not northern Finland, Sweden and Norway

Nickerl's Fritillary

♂♀

This fritillary has dusky dark wings, patterned with orange and brown. You can tell the females by their larger size and even darker colouring. Underneath the hindwing, a row of reddish marks runs along behind the margin. Look for Nickerl's Fritillary in wet meadows, moors and bogs in the summer. The caterpillars feed on plaintain.

Species: *Mellicta aurelia*
Family: Nymphalidae
Size: Up to 32 mm
Flight period: One or two; from June/July
Distribution: Central and eastern Europe

Spotted Fritillary

♂♀

The name gives you a clue to the appearance of this butterfly – it is spotted all over, especially on the undersides of its wings. Above, the wings have an orange base. Underneath, they are paler in colour, with two orange bands crossing the hindwing. The Spotted Fritillary flies in flowery meadows, open woodland and heathland. Its caterpillars feed on plantain, toadflax, speedwell and other plants.

Species: *Melitaea didyma*
Family: Nymphalidae
Size: Up to 44 mm
Flight period: Three; flies between May and September
Distribution: Southern and central Europe eastwards

Knapweed Fritillary

This gaily patterned butterfly has orange and yellow wings speckled with black markings. The underside of the hindwing is pale yellow patterned with black and orange, and there is a band of red spots edged in black behind the margin. The Knapweed Fritillary is named after its caterpillar's foodplant, found in the flowery meadows where this butterfly lives.

Species: *Melitaea phoebe*
Family: Nymphalidae – Size: Up to 48 mm
Flight period: Three; flies between April and August
Distribution: Southern and central Europe eastwards

Glanville Fritillary

This butterfly was named after an enthusiastic British collector Lady Eleanor Glanville. It has busily patterned wings with orange and black markings, and the undersides have beige and orange bands with small black dots. The Glanville Fritillary can be found in flowery meadows, where they sunbathe and drink nectar from wild flowers. The caterpillars are black and spiny, and feed on the leaves of sea plantain and ribwort plantain and knapweed.

Species: *Melitaea cinxia*
Family: Nymphalidae – Size: Up to 40 mm
Flight period: Two; flies between May and September
Distribution: Western Europe eastwards

Olive Skipper

You can't see the reason for this butterfly's name unless you look under the wings. Above, they are dark brown, with a few whitish marks and chequered fringes. Underneath, though, the wings are olive-green, with larger marks in white. The Olive Skipper flies in meadows on the sides of mountains, during the summer months.

Species: *Pyrgus serratulae*
Family: Hesperiidae – Size: Up to 28 mm
Flight period: One; flies between July and August
Distribution: Spain, north, central and southeastern Europe

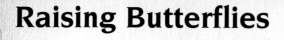

Raising Butterflies

A good way to learn more about butterflies is to rear them yourself, from caterpillars. Look for caterpillars in the spring and summer on leaves, stems and grasses. It is very important that your caterpillars have enough food, otherwise they will starve to death.

It's easy to find the right food – just make a note of where you found the caterpillar and what the plant was, so you can return and collect more when you need it. (Take a stalk of the plant with some leaves if you are not sure you will recognize it again).

Rearing cages

Caterpillar-rearing cages are available from special stores, otherwise you can easily make your own. You could use:

- a card shoebox covered with window screening on top
- a sheet of clear plastic rolled into a tube standing in a plastic tub with soil in the bottom
- a large clear jar (1 litre or more)

For the last two, cover the top with cheesecloth and secure it with an elastic band.

How to rear caterpillars

1 **When you have found some caterpillars, break off the piece of the plant** you found them on and gently place it in your prepared container. When the caterpillars are newly hatched and tiny, they don't need a big cage. A jar or plastic box lined with newspaper will do.
2 **Remember that your caterpillars will need new leaves EVERY day.**
3 **When they grow bigger** (after their first moult,) you will need to transfer the caterpillars to a more suitable container (see above). Be careful! Move your caterpillars using the tip of a small paintbrush. This will help you to avoid damaging them, and it stops them damaging you (some caterpillars have stinging hairs). Place them on their food plant in the new cage.

4 **Now you can pick bigger bits of the food plant, and place them in a jar of water to keep them fresh.** Put a twig or stick in too, for perching, and for the caterpillars to hang from when they pupate. Make sure you plug up the top of the jar with cotton to stop the growing caterpillars from falling into the water. Keep putting fresh plants in every other day.

5 **Caterpillars may take a while to turn into chrysalises** – and sometimes they have to spend the winter in the chrysalis. If they go very still, leave them alone in a cool place until the spring.

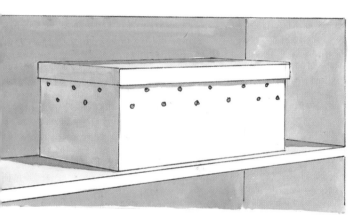

6 **Remember to label the caterpillars' or pupae's box** with the date, species name, etc.

7 **If the caterpillars pupate in soil or sand, spray the soil occasionally with water** as it must be damp – otherwise the pupae might die.

8 **When the adult butterflies have struggled out of the chrysalis,** remove the top of the cage and put it outside. They will only fly away when their wings have dried and expanded.

What to watch for

When you are rearing your caterpillars, make notes of the following things. Also, try sketching the different stages in the butterfly's life as they occur.

- What is the name of the food plant you found your caterpillars on?
- How many times do the caterpillars moult?
- Do any of the caterpillars make a leaf tent?
- How long do the caterpillars take to turn into chrysalises?
- What are the chrysalises like? Can you see the butterfly's wings through the skin, and at what stage?
- How long does it take for the butterfly to break out of the chrysalis skin?
- How long does it take the butterfly to dry? And to pump up its wings?
- Can you identify the butterfly?

Meadows

Twin-spot Fritillary

This butterfly gets its name from the two rows of black spots that follow the margins of all its wings above and below. The wings are reddish orange with dark margins and various other markings in black. Undersides have yellow marks, and the hindwing has a black-edged yellow band. The Twin-spot Fritillary flies in flowery meadows and slopes in the summer.

Species: *Brenthis hecate*
Family: Nymphalidae
Size: Up to 44 mm
Flight period: One; flies between May and June
Distribution: Southwestern Europe eastwards

Niobe Fritillary

This butterfly has rounded wings, which are orange and patterned with black marks. There is a wavy black line behind the dark margins of all wings. Underneath the hindwing is the best identification feature: a single black centred spot near the base. Here, too, there is a green tinge and big silver marks edged in black veins. The Niobe Fritillary flies in flowery meadows in the summer. Here, its caterpillars feed on violet leaves.

Species: *Fabriciana niobe*
Family: Nymphalidae
Size: Up to 60 mm
Flight period: One; flies between June and July
Distribution: Most of western Europe

Spanish Festoon

This butterfly is easy to spot, with its garish yellow, black and red pattern. Clear, wavy, black margins adorn the edges of all the wings, and there is a white mark on each forewing. Underneath, the wings have a pink flush. The Spanish Festoon flies in wet meadows where birthwort grows. This is its caterpillar's foodplant.

Species: *Zerynthia rumina*
Family: Papilionidae
Size: Up to 46 mm
Flight period: One; flies between February and May
Distribution: Southwestern Europe

Queen of Spain Fritillary

This handsome butterfly is difficult to miss. Its pointed wings are brightly patterned on top with orange-gold and black marks, and underneath they are covered in big silver blotches on a light background. These make the butterfly sparkle in the sunshine, as it flits from flower to flower sipping nectar. Look for the Queen of Spain Fritillary in flowery meadows and pastures, in sunny woodland glades and along paths. Caterpillars, which are black and spiny, feed on violet leaves.

Species: *Argynnis lathonia*
Family: Nymphalidae – Size: Up to 46 mm
Flight period: Three; flies between March and October
Distribution: Southern Europe often migrating northwards

Sooty Copper

This butterfly is so-called because of the sooty colour of the males' wings, which also have some orange marks running round the edges. Females, by contrast, have orange forewings, and sooty hindwings, with larger orange marks dotted in black. The undersides are lemon yellow and speckled in black, and have an orange band running along the edge. The Sooty Copper flies in flowery meadows.

Species: *Heodes tityrus*
Family: Lycaenidae – Size: Up to 32 mm
Flight period: Two; flies between April and September
Distribution: Spain, eastwards through Europe

Lesser Spotted Fritillary

This butterfly has deep orange-red wings with rows of black markings. The undersides of the hindwings are mustard yellow, with triangular black marks around the margin. The Lesser Spotted Fritillary lives in flowery meadows.

Species: *Melitaea trivia*
Family: Nymphalidae – Size: Up to 38 mm
Flight period: Two; flies between May and August
Distribution: Southern Europe

Meadows

Duke of Burgundy Fritillary

This butterfly is called 'fritillary' because its pattern is like that of fritillaries, not because it is part of their family. The wings are dark brown with red-orange spots and a broken white fringe around the wings. Females have more red colour than males. Underneath the hindwings there are two rows of white marks. The Duke of Burgundy Fritillary is a fast flier, darting around flowery meadows and woodland clearings, especially where the caterpillar's foodplants, cowslips and primroses, grow. It also likes to sunbathe on low-growing vegetation or on bare earth.

Species: *Hamearis lucina* – **Family:** Riodinidae
Size: Up to 28 mm – **Flight period:** One in the North; two in the South; flies between May and August
Distribution: Central Spain to central Europe and eastwards

Lesser Marbled Fritillary

This is a smaller version of the Marbled Fritillary. Its wings are rounded with dark marks against an orange background and dark margins. The undersides of the wings are paler, and the hindwing has broken yellow marks, as well as a touch of green and orange towards the bottom. Look for the Lesser Marbled Fritillary in wet meadows and hollows, during June and July. Its caterpillars feed on meadowsweet, raspberry and great burnet.

Species: *Brenthis ino* – **Family:** Nymphalidae
Size: Up to 40 mm
Flight period: One; flies between June and July
Distribution: Central and northern Europe

Bog Fritillary

You'll find this little butterfly in North America as well as Europe. Its wings are rust-orange with fine black lines and dots, and zigzag marks along the margins. Underneath, the hindwings have a row of black-rimmed pearly spots along the margin. Its favourite habitat is given away by its name – bogs, wet meadows and marshes. Here, it hides among mosses and heather if the sun is not out. Its caterpillars feed on bistort, violets and willows.

Species: *Proclossiana eunomia*
Family: Nymphalidae – **Size:** Up to 46 mm
Flight period: One; flies between June and July
Distribution: Scattered in western Europe

Pearl-bordered Fritillary

You can only see the reason for this butterfly's name if you look at its undersides. Above, the wings are orange with dark lines and dots. But underneath the hindwings, a string of seven silvery-white dots or 'pearls' decorate the margins. This butterfly lives in woodland glades and meadows, fluttering around wild flowers drinking nectar. It likes to sunbathe too, and rests under grasses at night. Caterpillars find their foodplant, violets, along woodland paths and in clearings.

Species: *Boloria euphrosyne*
Family: Nymphalidae
Size: Up to 46 mm
Flight period: Two; flies between April and August
Distribution: Most of Europe, except southern Spain, and most of Ireland

False Comma

This butterfly has tortoiseshell patterns and orange-red, brown and black colouring. There are white marks at the top edges of the forewings and hindwings, and the forewings have the most black markings. The edges of the wings are rather ragged, and the undersides are brown, forming excellent camouflage against tree bark. The False Comma lives in flowery meadows, often near woodland. The caterpillars feed on elm and the leaves of other deciduous trees.

Species: *Nymphalis vau-album*
Family: Nymphalidae – Size: Up to 66 mm
Flight period: One; flies between July and September
Distribution: Eastern Europe

Scarce Copper

Male and female Scarce Coppers look completely different. The males have plain coppery wings, with dark margins. Females have orange forewings, liberally patterned with black spots, and dark hindwings with an orange border. The undersides are light tan. The Scarce Copper flies in flowery meadows and along waysides. Its caterpillars feed on dock leaves.

Species: *Heodes virgaureae*
Family: Lycaenidae
Size: Up to 36 mm
Flight period: One; flies between July and August
Distribution: Spain to Finland, Sweden and Norway

Purple-shot Copper

This butterfly gets its name from the purple sheen to the male's forewings, which contrasts with the orange hindwings. Females have brown wings with an orange band around the hindwing. Males and females have some faint dark spots on their wings. Underneath, the wings are grey-orange and speckled with black spots. The Purple-shot Copper flies in flowery meadows in the summer, and its caterpillars feed on dock.

Species: *Heodes alciphron*
Family: Lycaenidae – Size: Up to 36 mm
Flight period: One; flies between June and July
Distribution: Western Europe eastwards

Meadows

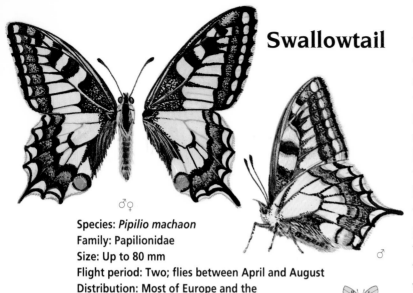

Swallowtail

This big, handsome butterfly is unmistakable. The wings are black and yellow, with red and blue eyespots on the hindwings, and a blue band along the hindwing margin. The colours and pattern are repeated on the underside. The name 'Swallowtail' comes from the 'tails' on each hindwing which look like a swallow's tail. Together with the eyespot, the tail confuses predators as to where the butterfly's head is! Caterpillars also have their tricks. At first, they resemble bird droppings, and then, when fully grown, they can display a pair of orange horns to frighten attackers; they also give off odours! They feed on milk parsley, found in the meadows, wetlands and mountain pastures where the Swallowtails fly.

Species: *Pipilio machaon*
Family: Papilionidae
Size: Up to 80 mm
Flight period: Two; flies between April and August
Distribution: Most of Europe and the Norfolk Broads in England

---

Scarce Swallowtail

The name of this butterfly is misleading. In fact, it is much more common than the ordinary Swallowtail. You can tell it from the latter by its larger size, paler colouring, and the six vertical black stripes on the forewings. The tails are also longer and have a white tip. When on the wing, the tails give the impression that it is flying backwards, which confuses predators and makes it hard to attack. A strong flier, the Scarce Swallowtail can be spotted in meadows, pastures, around farmland and in orchards. Its caterpillars feed on the leaves of hawthorn, blackthorn, cherry and other fruit trees.

Species: *Iphiclides podalirius*
Family: Papilionidae
Size: Up to 90 mm
Flight period: Two; flies between March and September
Distribution: Most of Europe, except Britain, Denmark, and Sweden

Southern Festoon

This pretty butterfly has black, red and blue markings against a yellow background. There is a zigzag pattern in black edging all the wings, and red spots on the hindwing. Underneath, the pattern is repeated. There are no tails. The Southern Festoon flies in wet meadows where its caterpillars' foodplant, birthwort, grows.

Species: *Zerynthia polyxena*
Family: Papilionidae – **Size:** Up to 52 mm
Flight period: One; flies between April and May
Distribution: Southeastern Europe

♂♀

Berger's Clouded Yellow

This butterfly is similar to the Pale Clouded Yellow, but the males' wings are a brighter yellow. They also have dark forewing tips, and there is an orange spot in the hindwing. Females have greenish white wings with dark forewing tips filled with white spots, and also an orange spot in the hindwing. Berger's Clouded Yellow flies in flowery meadows on downs. Caterpillars, which are yellow and black, feed on tufted horseshoe vetch.

Species: *Colias australis*
Family: Pieridae – **Size:** Up to 54 mm
Flight period: Two; flies between May and September
Distribution: Southern and Central Europe to 54°N, most common in the Southwest

Pale Clouded Yellow

Males seem to suit this butterfly's name better than females. They have pale yellow wings, with black forewing tips filled with lighter spots. Females are off-white with black forewing tips, also spotted with white. The only yellow on their wings is a spot in the middle of each hindwing. The Pale Clouded Yellow flies in flowery meadows. The caterpillars feed on lucerne and clover leaves.

♂♀   ♂

Species:
Colias hyale
Family:
Pieridae
Size: Up to 50 mm
Flight period: Two; flies between May and September
Distribution: Central Europe from 60°N, commoner in the North and East, migrant to 65°N, absent from Spain and Italy

♂

Meadow Fritillary

Males and females of this butterfly look very different. The males have red-orange wings, with dark markings and a dark border. Females' wings are yellow-brown, with red-orange spots on the forewing edges, as well as dark markings and borders. Underneath the hindwing, there is a row of orange spots, as well as a row of pale yellow marks crossing the wing. The Meadow Fritillary can be found in flowery meadows, in moors and in bogs.

Species: *Mellicta parthenoides*
Family: Nymphalidae
Size: Up to 36 mm
Flight period: Two; flies between June and July
Distribution: Western Europe

♂♀

Purple-edged Copper

The males give the name to this butterfly. They have bright red-orange wings, bordered in purple. Females have orange forewings with black dots, and dark hindwings with an orange margin. The undersides are pale brown with black spots, and orange on the female forewing. The Purple-edged Copper flies in wet meadows in the summer. The caterpillars feed on dock leaves.

Species: *Palaeochrysophanus hippothoe*
Family: Lycaenidae
Size: Up to 38 mm
Flight period: One; flies between June and July
Distribution: Central and southern Europe

♂♀   ♂

Meadows

Bath White

About 1795, this butterfly was identified from a piece of embroidery done by a young girl from Bath. Since then it has been known as the Bath White. The wings are white with black marks on the forewing tips in both males and females. Females have black marks on the hindwings as well. The real key is the undersides, which are mottled with green. Look for the Bath White flying in fields and meadows which are rich in wild flowers and clover. Caterpillars are bluish-grey with raised black dots and yellow stripes. They feed on the leaves of rockcress, mustard, mignonette and similar plants.

♂♀   ♂

Species: *Pontia daplidice*
Family: Pieridae
Size: Up to 50 mm
Flight period: Two; flies between February and September
Distribution: South and central Europe, as a migrant

Black-veined White

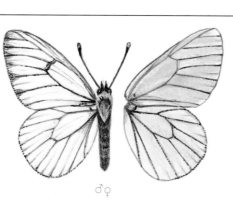

♂♀

This butterfly is easy to recognize with its plain white wings crossed with clear black veins. The scales on the wings do not last very long, as the courtship ritual involves wing-rubbing. Look for the Black-veined White flying over clover meadows, up mountains and in orchards. It was once a pest to fruit trees, as its caterpillars fed on the leaves of apples and plums. They also like to feed on hawthorn, blackthorn and cherry tree leaves.

Species: *Aporia crategi*
Family: Pieridae
Size: Up to 68 mm
Flight period: One; flies between May and June
Distribution: Most of Europe except Britain and extreme northern Europe

Dappled White

This butterfly has white wings with black forewing tips, and a black mark in the centre of each forewing. The undersides of the wings are green, with uneven white spots. Females are larger than the males. Look for the Dappled White flying in flowery, sub-alpine meadows.

♂♀   ♂

Species: *Euchloe simponia*
Family: Pieridae
Size: Up to 48 mm
Flight period: Two; flies between March and June
Distribution: Southwestern and southeastern Europe

Danube Clouded Yellow

As the name suggests, this butterfly lives mainly along the River Danube. The male has rich orange wings, edged with thick dark borders, thickest on the forewings. Females are a paler orange colour, and their dark margins have a row of yellow marks in them. The undersides are orange. The Danube Clouded Yellow flies in flowery meadows.

Species: *Colias myrmidone* – **Family: Pieridae**
Size: Up to 50 mm
Flight period: Two; flies between May and August
Distribution: Central and southeastern Europe

Clouded Yellow

Males and females of this butterfly have bright orange-yellow wings with a broad dark border and an orange spot in the centre of each hindwing. You can tell the females by the yellow spots within the border. The Clouded Yellow is a rapid flier, darting around flowery meadows and sipping nectar from wild flowers. Caterpillars, which are green, feed on vetches and other members of the pea family.

Species: *Colias croceus*
Family: Pieridae
Size: Up to 54 mm
Flight period: Several; flies between April and September
Distribution: Throughout most of Europe in spring

Orange Tip

Only the males of this butterfly boast the orange tip, found on the edge of the forewings, and edged in black. The rest of the wings are white, and females have black wingtips. Males and females have mottled green undersides, which is a good identification tool. Look for Orange Tips flying along roadsides, and in flowery meadows. Caterpillars feed on creeping yellow-cress, cuckoo flower, large bittercress, wild turnip and garlic mustard.

Species: *Anthocaris cardamines*
Family: Pieridae
Size: Up to 48 mm
Flight period: Two; flies between March and April
Distribution: Most of Europe, except the extreme north and south

Moroccan Orange Tip

Not only found in Morocco, this beautiful butterfly lives up to its name with its orange-tipped forewings. Males are by far the brightest, with their lime-yellow wings, each with a vivid orange patch. Their hindwing undersides are deep yellow with black marks. Females are white, with a brown-orange forewing tip. The underside of the hindwing is pale yellow with greenish areas. Look for the Moroccan Orange Tip in flowery waysides and meadows, where its caterpillars find their foodplant, buckler mustard.

Species: *Anthocaris belia*
Family: Pieridae – Size: Up to 40 mm
Flight period: One; flies between May and July
Distribution: Portugal to Italy and Switzerland

Butterfly Garden

If you have a garden, you can do a lot to make it attractive to butterflies. This will help the butterflies and will also make your garden a very colourful place. The best way to start is to grow flowers that have lots of nectar. Many butterflies love to sip this with their long tongues, which are a bit like straws. Trees, too, can attract butterflies – some species like to drink tree sap, or eat rotten fruit on the ground.

Don't forget about the caterpillars – if you grow their food plants, it will encourage female butterflies to lay their eggs there. Another important thing to remember is not to use insecticide sprays in your garden. These can kill butterflies as well as pests.

Butterfly watching

Watching how butterflies and caterpillars behave in the field can be interesting and exciting. You can get a really good look at them if they are busy feeding or drinking, so a flowery garden is one of the best places to start. Approach the butterfly quietly and be careful not to make any sudden movements – this will frighten it away.

Caterpillars can't fly away, but they can look like something else – such as leaves, twigs, or even bird droppings. You'll need to look extra carefully for these. Beware of hairy caterpillars – they can give you a nasty rash.

Flowers & trees

Adult butterflies will feed on lots of different flowers. Most prefer certain colours like pink, mauve and purple. Large butterflies prefer to feed from tall flowers, while smaller types like low-growing flowers. Butterflies also like flowers with flat tops or large petals that are easy to land on. If you let a piece of your garden go wild, the wild flowers and weeds that grow there will also attract butterflies.

Nettles: Red Admirals lay their eggs on nettles, as this is their caterpillars' food plant.

Daisies: Don't get rid of your daisies – butterflies like the Comma sip their nectar.

Clover: These are food plants for many types of caterpillars.

Other good flowering plants are sunflowers, lilacs, passion flowers, pansies, marigolds and rock roses.

Buddleia: The flowers that this shrub produces are so popular with butterflies that it is often called the butterfly bush. The Peacock is a good example of a buddleia-loving butterfly.

The leaves of trees are food plants for many types of caterpillars. Favourite trees include: oak, birch, willow, sycamore, cherry, and poplar.

When is a butterfly not a butterfly?

When it's a moth, of course! There are even more moths than butterflies around (well over 100,000 species worldwide,) but as a general rule, they are not so noticeable. This is the way you tell them apart, but remember there are exceptions to all these tests:

- Butterflies fly during the day; moths fly at night.
- Butterflies are brightly coloured; moths are usually drably coloured.
- Butterflies rest with their wings held vertically; moths rest with them held flat.
- The antennae of most butterflies end in small clubs (see page 6).

Mountains

High up in the clouds, often wind-swept and cold, mountains also seem like unlikely butterfly homes. And it is true that the butterflies that live here have to be hardy. The weather often changes quickly from sunny and tranquil to windy and snowy.

When the sun is out, mountain butterflies make the most of it: they sunbathe with their wings outstretched. They often have dark-coloured wings to absorb the heat quickly. Hairy bodies also help to keep in the precious warmth should the weather change suddenly. Notice the way that butterflies of these areas fly – close to the ground and in short bursts. This is to combat the fierce winds that often sweep over mountain tops. This picture shows five species from this section; how many can you recognize?

Apollo, Dryad, Hermit, Painted Lady, Sooty Ringlet.

Mountain Small White

The name does not leave us guessing much about this butterfly! It is small, mostly white, and lives on mountainsides. The wings of the female are slightly darker than those of the male. Both males and females have dark marks on the forewings. Look for the Mountain Small White on flowery slopes, where plenty of wild crucifers (mustard, wallflower, etc) grow. This is its caterpillar's foodplant.

Species: *Pieris ergane* – **Family:** Pieridae – **Size:** Up to 40 mm
Flight period: Two; flies between March and September
Distribution: Southeastern to southwestern Europe

Peak White

On top, this butterfly's wings are white, with grey and black marks. Underneath, they have thick green veins, which actually show through to the front. You can tell the females by the even white darts running down the edge of the forewing, outlined in black. The Peak White is so called because of its preference for mountain peaks. It flies in the summer, in flowery alpine meadows, where its caterpillars feed on wild crucifers.

Species: *Pontia daplidice* – **Family:** Pieridae – **Size:** Up to 52 mm
Flight period: Two; flies between June and July/August
Distribution: Alps and Pyrenees

Clouded Apollo

This butterfly is much smaller than the Apollo, and has a tell-tale indentation on its hindwings. The wings are off-white, with some black marks and spots, stronger in the males. Look for the Clouded Apollo in mountain meadows and woodland glades in the summer.

Species: *Parnassius mnemosyne*
Family: Papilionidae
Size: Up to 62 mm
Flight period: One;
flies between May and July
Distribution: Much of central and southern Europe

Apollo

This is a large, handsome and easily recognizable butterfly. It has big wings with rounded edges. Against a white background, there are black spots and markings on the forewings, and red and black spots on the hindwings. The wings may sometimes feel greasy, and the bodies and base of wings are often very hairy. The Apollo flies slowly through alpine meadows and pastures, making it easy for collectors to catch. The caterpillars are velvety black with a line of orange-red spots along their sides. They feed on the leaves of stonecrop and sempervivum.

Species:
Parnassius apollo
Family: Papilionidae
Size: Up to 80 mm
Flight period:
One; flies between
June and September
Distribution:
Mountainous areas
of Europe

Mountains

Rock Grayling

This is a very dark coloured butterfly. The wings are chocolate-brown with a wide light band running vertically down the wings. There are two eyespots of different sizes on the forewings, and they have black 'pupils' in the middle. This butterfly is called the Rock Grayling because it can be found around rocky outcrops of mountains. The caterpillars feed on grasses.

Species:
Hipparchia alcyone
Family: Satyridae
Size: Up to 68 mm
Flight period: One; flies between June and July
Distribution: Central and southeastern Europe

Tree Grayling

The dark colour of this grayling makes it hard to notice. Against a dark brown background, there are two tiny white marks and two black eyespots on the forewings. Females have some small brown spots on their hindwings as well. Underneath, the wings are mottled light grey-brown, which is good for hiding them against trees. Look for the Tree Grayling in woodland, and on mountains, hills and heaths. Caterpillars feed on grasses.

Species: *Neohipparchia* – **Family: Satyridae** – **Size: Up to 46 mm**
Flight period: One; fies between July and September
Distribution: Spain and Portugal through central and southern Europe eastwards

Dryad

Male Dryads have dark brown wings, with two blue-pupilled eyespots on the forewings, and one on the hindwings. Females are larger and lighter in colour, and their eyespots are clearer and surrounded by pale yellow rings. Underneath, males and females have large eyespots on the forewings. The Dryad flies on grassy slopes in mountain areas, and its caterpillars feed on grasses.

Species: *Minois dryas* – **Family: Satyridae** – **Size: Up to 70 mm**
Flight period: One; flies between July and August
Distribution: Central Europe

Silky Ringlet

♂   ♀

This butterfly is brown, with a wide band of orange crossing the forewing and part of the hindwing vertically. In males, the band is red-orange with two black eyespots with white pupils. In females, the band is lighter orange with an extra spot on the forewing and four more spots on the hindwing. Underneath, the forewings are yellow-brown, with two eyespots, and the hindwings are mottled grey-brown. The Silky Ringlet flies on rocky slopes in mountains. Its caterpillars feed on grasses.

Species: *Erebia gorge* – **Family:** Satyridae – **Size:** Up to 40 mm
Flight period: One; flies between June and July
Distribution: Scattered through central and southern Europe

Mountain Ringlet

This dark coloured butterfly has dark brown wings crossed by a red-orange band across the forewing. Within this band are black spots. There are also some orange spots around the hindwing margin. The underside hindwing is pale brown, while the forewing has an orange base. It is found in mountainous, often boggy areas, where it flies close to the ground. Look for this butterfly in sunny weather in alpine grassy meadows. When the sun goes in, it hides in the grass. Caterpillars feed on grasses – especially mat and wavy-haired grasses.

Species: *Erebia epiphron* – **Family:** Satyridae
Size: Up to 38 mm – **Flight period:** One; flies between June and August – **Distribution:** Mountains of central and southern Europe, including Britain

♀

♂♀

Hermit

This butterfly has brown wings crossed by a white-cream band running vertically down each side. There are two dark spots on the forewings, but these are more definite in the female, and they also have white 'pupils'. Females can also be recognized by their larger size. The Hermit flies in rocky places and along rocky paths.

Species: *Chazara briseis*
Family: Satyridae
Size: Up to 60 mm
Flight period: One; flies between June and July
Distribution: Spain to southeastern and central Europe

♂♀

Great Sooty Satyr

The name 'Sooty' suits the males of this butterfly much better than the females. Males have very dark brown wings with two black, white-pupilled eyespots on the forewings. Females are orange-brown, with two much larger pupilled eyespots on their forewings, as well as one on the hindwing. Look for the Great Sooty Satyr in the summer, flying on mountain slopes and tracks. The caterpillars feed on tufted hair-grass, plentiful in these areas.

Species: *Satyrus ferula*
Family: Satyridae
Size: Up to 60 mm
Flight period: One; flies between July and August – **Distribution:** Southern Europe rarely north of 47°N; there is a colony in the East Pyrenees at Val d'Aran

♂♀

Mountains

Marbled Skipper

♂♀   ♂

This butterfly is so-called because of the marbled pattern on its wings, which are light greenish with white marks on fore- and hindwings. The undersides of the wings are pale green with very light bands, and the hindwings have a scalloped margin. The Marbled Skipper lives in flowery areas of slopes. Here, its caterpillars feed on woundwort.

Species: *Carcharodus lavatherae*
Family: Hesperiidae
Size: Up to 28 mm
Flight period: Two; flies between May and August
Distribution: Central and southern Europe

Tufted Marbled Skipper

This butterfly's name tells you a lot about its appearance. It has hair tufts on the underside of its hindwings, and its pattern on top is marbled with green, white, orange and black. Underneath, the hindwings are greenish with white marks, and the forewings are brownish. This skipper flies on flowery slopes, and its caterpillars' foodplant is white horehound.

Species: *Carcharodus flocciferus*
Family: Hesperiidae – Size: Up to 32 mm
Flight period: Two; flies between May and September
Distribution: Spain across southern Europe to Bulgaria

♂♀   ♂

Hungarian Skipper

As the name hints, this butterfly can be found in Eastern Europe. The Hungarian Skipper has brown wings, with a fine line of white dashes inside the margins. Underneath, the wings are pale olive-green with large white spots. It flies on flowery slopes, where its caterpillars feed on burnets and cinquefoil.

Species: *Spiala orbifer*
Family: Hesperiidae
Size: Up to 30 mm
Flight period: Two; flies between April and August
Distribution: Eastern Europe

♂♀   ♂

Chequered Blue

This butterfly has two 'chequered' areas. There are chequered fringes on its wings, and its undersides have an overall chequered pattern. Above, the males have dark blue forewings with a brown margin and brown hindwings. Females are brown with dark markings. The undersides of the wings are grey-white covered in large blocks of black. The hindwing also has a row of orange half-moon shapes. The Chequered Blue flies on rocky ground in the summer. Its caterpillars feed on stonecrop.

♂♀   ♂

Species: *Scolitantides orion*
Family: Lycaenidae
Size: Up to 32 mm
Flight period: One; flies between June and July
Distribution: Two distinct areas: Spain eastwards through southern Europe; Finland, Sweden and Norway

Painted Lady

This big, handsome butterfly has pointed forewings with black tips filled with white marks. There are also orange marks on the forewings, and the hindwings are orange and brown with a row of black spots and dashes around the margin. The undersides of the wings are rosy on the forewing and have a marbled pattern on the hindwing, with five eyespots. It can also be recognized by its flight – very fast and powerful, covering large distances. It flies over meadows, hedgerows and gardens, settling to sip nectar. Caterpillars feed on the leaves of thistles, mallows, burdock and stinging nettles.

Species: *Cynthia cardui* – **Family: Nymphalidae**
Size: Up to 70 mm
Flight period: Three; flies between
April and October as a migrant
Distribution: Most of Europe.
One of the world's most widespread butterflies

Spanish Purple Hairstreak

This butterfly has dark brown wings, and males boast a substantial purple area on their forewings. Females only have a little purple on their wings. Underneath, the wings are very different, light tan, with spotted orange borders. The hindwings have scalloped edges. This hairstreak is common in Spain, where it flies in woodland areas in mountains. Caterpillars feed on ash leaves.

Species: *Laesopis roboris* – **Family: Lycaenidae**
Size: Up to 30 mm
Flight period: One; flies between May and July
Distribution: Portugal, Spain and southeastern France

Sooty Ringlet

The very sooty-black wings of the males give this butterfly its name. Sometimes these black wings have two tiny pupilled spots on the forewings and two on the hindwing. Females have dark brown wings, with a very faint lighter brown band running down them. Underneath, the wings are sooty and plain. The Sooty Ringlet lives in mountainous areas, where its caterpillars can feed on sparse-growing meadow grasses.

Species: *Erebia pluto* – **Family: Satyridae** – **Size: Up to 50 mm**
Flight period: One; flies between June and August
Distribution: Alps and Apennines

Keeping Records

You might like to keep a diary recording when and where you find your butterflies. Always take your field notebook with you when you go butterfly hunting. Make sketches of the the butterflies you see for your diary, and take photographs of the area.

Butterfly diary

Keep your diary in a ring binder or a lever-arch file on separate sheets of paper. Fill out a sheet for each butterfly-hunting trip you go on with the details from your field notebook.

You can also write notes in it when you visit museums, or see a television programme about butterflies. You can decorate it with your own drawings, photographs, pictures from magazines, postcards and so on.

Butterfly walk

A good way to find out about butterflies in your neighbourhood is by making a regular 'butterfly walk'. This is how to do it:

1   **Plan a route that takes about one hour to walk** (about 4–5 km). Make sure it takes you past the different habitats in your neighbourhood (like fields, woods, lakes, parks, etc).

2   **Try to take this walk once a week** during the warmest time of the day and to do it in about one hour on each occasion. Try not to do it when the weather is wet or windy.

3   **Take your field notebook and this guidebook each time.**

4   **Record each butterfly** that comes within five metres of you, and how many there are.

Keeping a record

You can also record each species of butterfly that you see in a card index. The file should have a card for each species that gives detailed information like:

- the butterfly's common name, and its Latin name if known
- the family to which it belongs
- the date you saw it
- where you saw it: name and description of place
- the type of habitat
- the weather on the day of your visit
  You may be able to store your information on a computer. Keep an up-to-date printout, as well as your disk and its back-up.

5 **If you have to stop and identify a butterfly you don't recognize**, don't worry. Make a note of the time it takes you to identify the butterfly and add that time to the one hour your walk should take.

6 **Record your weekly information in a separate part of your butterfly diary.** Over the weeks, you will see which areas are best for butterflies and which species are most common at what time of year. Does your local pattern match the flight time information in this book?

Make a butterfly kite

Butterflies are so beautiful, they have inspired artists for centuries. Thousands of years ago, kite-makers in China made butterfly kites to flutter in the wind. You can make your own butterfly kite with some strong paper, two straws, some thin string, Sellotape, and paints or markers.

1 **Draw an outline of a butterfly on a piece of paper.** Colour in the wings with your paints or markers, giving them whatever pattern you like.

2 **When dry, cut the shape out from the paper,** being careful to keep it in one piece.

3 **Make some antennae from the string** and glue them to the butterfly's head.

4 **Place a long piece of string against the butterfly's body.** Lay the straws diagonally across the wings, on top of the string.

5 **Tape the straws down firmly** on to each of the four wing tips.

6 **Tie the string and the straws together** over the middle of the butterfly. Now your kite is ready to fly!

Woodlands

The woodland habitat includes two quite different types of woods. Deciduous, broad-leaved woods and forests are made up of trees that lose their leaves in winter, such as oak, beech, and ash. These trees have broad, flat leaves. Coniferous woods and forests are green all year round, and include pines, firs, cypresses and cedars. These trees have needle-like leaves.

Coniferous forests, which occur mostly in the northern parts of Europe, have few flowers growing on their floors because their thickly-packed branches let in so little sunshine. But some butterflies like to feed on pine needles, so this lack of flowers does not matter to them.

Deciduous woodlands and forests are more common in the rest of Europe. They let in plenty of light during the springtime to allow lots of wild flowers to grow on their floors. Here, you'll find butterflies drinking nectar, or resting on twigs and branches in sunny clearings (gaps among the trees). Don't forget to look for caterpillars munching on leaves and plants as well.

Clearings are found in both types of forest. They can be caused by the fall of a great tree that is at the end of its life, or by the actions of humans. The gap in the forest roof lets in sunlight and fast-growing plants take advantage of this before the slower-growing saplings shoot up to fill the hole. This picture shows four species from this section; how many can you recognize?

White Admiral, Black-eyed Blue, Brown Hairstreak, Purple Hairstreak.

Woodlands

Woodland Grayling

This big butterfly is ideally coloured for its woodland habitat. On top, the wings are brown, with a wide, lighter area towards the margins, and eyespots on the forewings. In females, this is yellowish towards the forewing margin and the eyespots are stronger. Underneath, the hindwing has a wavy pattern very like bark and perfect for camouflage. Caterpillars of the Woodland Grayling feed on a grass called Yorkshire Fog.

Species: *Hipparchia fagi* – **Family:** Satryidae
Size: Up to 76 mm
Flight period: One; flies in June to August
Distribution: From France across central Europe

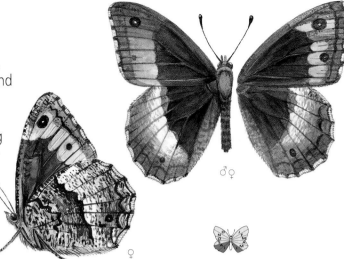

Purple Emperor

A big, spectacular butterfly, the Purple Emperor gets its name from the bright purple sheen on the male's wings. They also have a black border and white marks. Females have light brown wings with white marks. Underneath, the wings are patterned with orange, white and brown marks. They fly in clearings, mostly in the treetops, particularly among oak trees. Because of this, you'll find it hard to spot one, except in the morning sipping nectar from flowers on woodland paths. Caterpillars are fat and green – they feed on willow leaves.

Species: *Apatura iris* – **Family:** Nymphalidae
Size: Up to 75 mm
Flight period: One; flies between July and August
Distribution: Northern Spain to Baltic sea and central Europe

Lesser Purple Emperor

To confuse you, there are two colour forms of this butterfly. One has a yellowish brown tinge, while the other is similar to the Purple Emperor. In the latter form, males have the purple sheen on their wings, white markings and an orange-tipped black spot on the forewing. Females are brown, with white marks and orange and black spots on the forewing. The Lesser Purple Emperor flies along woodland paths and in clearings, where its caterpillars feed on poplar and willow leaves.

Species: *Apatura ilia*
Family: Nymphalidae
Size: Up to 70 mm
Flight period: Two; flies between May and September
Distribution: Central and southern Europe, but not Britain, Mediterranean lowlands or most of Spain

Black-eyed Blue

Males and females of this butterfly look slightly different. The males have plain blue wings with thin black margins. The females have blue wings too, but they have a lot of black in them seeping in from the margins and darkening the blue colour. Underneath, males and females have cream coloured wings, with a row of large black dots, especially on the forewings. The Black-eyed Blue flies on heaths and in woods in the spring. Its caterpillars feed on greenwood, leopard's bane and birdsfoot trefoil.

♂♀   ♀

Species: *Glaucopsyche melanops*
Family: Lycaenidae – **Size:** Up to 32 mm
Flight period: One; flies in April and May
Distribution: Spain, France and Italy

Iolas Blue

♂♀   ♂

Males of this large blue have violet-blue wings with thin dark margins. Females have darker blue wings with wider dark margins. Undersides are fawn with a row of white ringed black spots. The Iolas Blue flies in scrubby areas and in light woodland where its caterpillars can find their food plant, bladder senna.

Species: *Iolana iolas* – **Family:** Lycaenidae – **Size:** Up to 42 mm
Flight period: Two; flies between May and September
Distribution: Spain via southern Europe eastwards

Purple Hairstreak

♂♀   ♂

The name of this butterfly suits the males more than the females. They have bright purple all over their wings, with dark margins. Females have brown wings with just a small area of purple on the forewings. The undersides of males and females are the same, silvery grey with a white 'hairstreak', an orange spot and a tiny tail. There are also 'watermarks' on the margins of the hindwing. Purple Hairstreaks live in woodlands, but you'll have to look hard to find them, as they live in the tops of oak trees, rarely descending to a pathway or clearing. They are very territorial, and will attack any intruder. Rather than taking nectar from flowers, they sip honeydew left by aphids on leaves. Caterpillars feed mainly on oak leaves.

Species: *Quercusia quercus*
Family: Lycaenidae – **Size:** Up to 30 mm
Flight period: One; flies between July and August
Distribution: Most of Europe except northern Scandinavia

Common Glider

White bands cross the wings of this butterfly on a black background. The pattern is the same on the underside, although the hindwing has a reddish tinge. The Common Glider flies in woodlands and scrubby hillsides, glades and clearings. Its caterpillars are smooth with four pairs of spiny projections on the back; they eat spring pea.

Species: *Neptis sappho*
Family: Nymphalidae
Size: Up to 50 mm
Flight period: Two; flies between May and September
Distribution: Central and Eastern Europe

♂♀

Woodlands

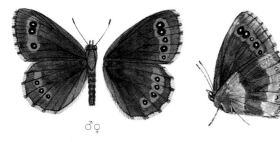

Scotch Argus

In the British Isles, the Scotch Argus lives mainly in Scotland, but elsewhere in Europe it is widespread. Dark brown wings crossed with orange bands are its trademark. The bands are filled with black, white-centred eyespots. This pattern is repeated on the forewing underside, and on the hindwing there is a grey band with small white dots. The Scotch Argus lives on woodland edges and in forest glades and rides. A sun-loving butterfly, you'll find it hard to spot one if the sun is not out. When at rest, the Scotch Argus looks like a withered leaf and so avoids attack. Caterpillars feed on grasses.

Species: *Erebia aethiops* – Family: Satyridae
Size: Up to 40 mm
Flight period: One; flies between August and September
Distribution: Scotland and central, southeastern and eastern Europe

Woodland Brown

This butterfly lives up to its name, as its wings are brown, and it lives in woodlands. The wings are large with scalloped, chequered margins and a row of yellow-ringed spots running vertically down each wing. Females have larger spots. On the underside, the pattern is repeated, with two yellow lines around the margin. The Woodland Brown lives on woodland margins, and in glades and clearings. Caterpillars feed on grasses.

Species: *Lopina achine*
Family: Satyridae
Size: Up to 56 mm
Flight period: One; flies between June and July
Distribution: Northern Spain eastwards

Large Ringlet

This big butterfly has rich brown wings with an orange band crossing them, filled with a row of black spots. Females are a bit bigger and their black spots have white pupils. Underneath, the pattern is the same but paler, with chequered margins. Look for the Large Ringlet flying on mountain slopes and in clearings and woodland in the summer. Caterpillars feed on different types of grasses.

Species: *Erebia euryale*
Family: Satyridae
Size: Up to 48 mm
Flight period: One; flies between July and August
Distribution: From northern Spain to southeastern Europe, via the Alps

Woodland Ringlet

This butterfly is brown, with a row of eyespots set in orange running down its wings. In males, this pattern is repeated very strongly on the underside. Females are similar, but larger and paler with larger eyespots above. The Woodland Ringlet flies on moors, and in meadows, bogs and light woodland. Caterpillars feed on finger grass and wood millet.

Species: *Erebia medusa*
Family: Satyridae
Size: Up to 48 mm
Flight period: One; flies between May and June
Distribution: Central and eastern Europe

Ilex Hairstreak

This butterfly is named after the food plant of its caterpillars, the holm or ilex oak. Males and females look different. The males have brown wings, with a small orange spot at the base of the hindwing. Females are brighter, with a large orange mark on the forewing as well. The hindwings have tails, and are crossed on the underside with a white hairstreak line and an orange band. The Ilex Hairstreak lives in woodland areas.

Species: *Nordmannia ilicis*
Family: Lycaenidae – **Size:** Up to 36 mm
Flight period: One; flies between June and July
Distribution: Southern and central Europe

False Ilex Hairstreak

Males and females of this butterfly both have rich brown wings. Females lack the bright orange mark of the Ilex Hairstreak, and have only a faint smudge on their forewings. There are tiny tails on the hindwings, and underneath, a row of orange spots around the margin. Look for this butterfly in light woodland and scrubby areas.

Species: *Nordmannia esculi*
Family: Lycaenidae
Size: Up to 34 mm
Flight period: One; flies between June and July
Distribution: Southwestern Europe

White-letter Hairstreak

You can only see the reason for this butterfly's name by looking on the underside hindwing. Here, there is a letter 'W' in white, as well as orange and black marks. Above, the wings are plain dark brown with tails on the hindwings. The White-letter Hairstreak lives in light woodland areas and around trees in towns. It sips nectar from bramble and privet blossom. Caterpillars feed on the leaves and flowers of elm trees. Dutch Elm Disease has had a devastating effect on this species, but it still survives.

Species: *Strymonidia w-album*
Family: Lycaenidae
Size: Up to 32 mm
Flight period: One; flies in July
Distribution: Northern Spain eastwards through Europe

Brown Hairstreak

Both males and females of this butterfly have brown wings with little tails on the hindwings. Females are much brighter however, with broad bands of orange crossing their forewings, as well as orange on the tails. Males only have orange on the tails. The Brown Hairstreak lives in woodlands and hedge trees, feeding on honeydew left on leaves by aphids. It is hard to spot, because it stays high in the treetops. Caterpillars feed on sloe, plum and birch leaves.

Species: *Thecla betulae*
Family: Lycaenidae
Size: Up to 36 mm
Flight period: One; flies between July and September – **Distribution:** Western and central Europe

Woodlands

Two-tailed Pasha

This large, handsome butterfly is easy to recognize
– if you can find one. It has big dark wings with
broad orange margins and blue marks on the
hindwing bases, repeated on the underside. There
are two pairs of unequal tails on each hindwing.
The Two-tailed Pasha is a powerful flier, and lives
in light woodlands, valleys and plains. It usually
stays high up in the treetops, but will come to
ground level to feed on rotting fruit. The
caterpillars feed on the leaves of
the strawberry tree.

Species: *Charaxes jasius*
Family: Nymphalidae – Size: Up to 82 mm
Flight period: Two; flies between May and September
Distribution: Mainly coastal, Mediterranean and Portugal

Hungarian Glider

This butterfly has dark wings with a single broad
white band crossing the hindwings, and random
white marks on the forewings. This pattern is
repeated on the undersides, but the background
colour here is reddish. The Hungarian Glider flies
along waysides and in woodlands. Its caterpillars
feed on meadowsweet.

Species: *Neptis revularis*
Family: Nymphalidae – Size: Up to 54 mm
Flight period: Two; flies between May and September
Distribution: Mainly coastal, Mediterranean and Portugal

White Admiral

This large butterfly has dark brown wings with a
white band running across the fore- and hindwings.
Underneath, the colours are much brighter, orange-
brown with a broad white band and various dark
dots and dashes. They can be seen in sunny glades
and pathways in woodlands, drinking nectar from
clumps of brambles. Caterpillars, which are dark
green with red spines, feed on honeysuckle leaves.

Species: *Ladoga camilla* **– Family: Nymphalidae**
Size: Up to 60 mm
Flight period: One; flies in June and July
Distribution: Central Europe

Map Butterfly

Can you see how this butterfly got its name? Its wings are crossed by map-like lines. They are patterned with dark marks on an orange-red background. Butterflies that appear in the second brood (or generation) look slightly different, darker and larger. Map Butterflies live in open woodland and along forest pathways. Females lay their eggs in long chains on the caterpillars' food plant, stinging nettle.

Species: *Araschnia levana*
Family: Nymphalidae – **Size:** Up to 40 mm
Flight period: Two; flies between May and September
Distribution: France, central Europe eastwards

Titania's Fritillary

This butterfly can be found in North America as well as Europe. It is dark orange with a very strong black pattern of dots, dashes, triangles and crescents. You can see the Titania's Fritillary in woodland glades and clearings. Caterpillars feed on bistort and violets.

Species: *Clossiana titania*
Family: Nymphalidae
Size: Up to 48 mm
Flight period: One; flies between June and July
Distribution: Central Europe, Baltic States

Chequered Skipper

This highly patterned skipper is easy to recognize. Above, it has large yellow spots on a brown background. The undersides have a similar pattern but are paler in colour. The Chequered Skipper lives in woodland clearings and edges, and along waysides. Caterpillars feed on brome grass and tor grass.

Species: *Carterocephalus palaemon*
Family: Hesperiidae
Size: Up to 30 mm
Flight period: One; flies between June and July
Distribution: Central to northern Europe; extinct in England

Pearly Heath

This butterfly gets its names from the pearly underside to its hindwing. Here, also, there is a row of ringed eyespots in a pale yellow band. Above, the wings are orange, with thick dark margins. Males have dusky hindwings, while females have more orange on theirs. There are also various eyespots on the upper wing surface. Pearly Heaths fly along flowery waysides and woodlands, and their caterpillars feed on grasses.

Species: *Coenonympha arcania*
Family: Satyridae
Size: Up to 40 mm
Flight period: Two; flies between June and August
Distribution: Western Europe eastwards

Woodlands

High Brown Fritillary

This large butterfly has orange wings with a dark pattern. Females are darker and larger than the males. Underneath the hindwings, a good recognition feature is a row of silver spots inside red markings. The High Brown Fritillary flutters in woodland glades and along flowery waysides, sipping nectar from bramble and thistle flowers. As the name suggests, it often flies high among the treetops, especially on dull days. Caterpillars feed on dog violet and sweet violet.

Species: *Argynnis adippe*
Family: Nymphalidae – Size: Up to 62 mm
Flight period: One; flies between June and August
Distribution: Most of Europe except extreme south

Brimstone

Only males gave this butterfly its name: 'brimstone' is an old word for sulphur, which is yellow. Males' bright yellow wings have a single orange dot in each fore- and hindwing. Females are pale green with the same orange spots. Brimstones fly along waysides, in woodland clearings and around buildings. Their caterpillars eat purging buckthorn and alder buckthorn.

Species: *Gonepteryx rhamni*
Family: Pieridae
Size: Up to 60 mm
Flight period: One; flies between April and September
Distribution: Most of Europe

Violet Fritillary

The Violet Fritillary is not named after its colour, but after its caterpillar's food plant, violets. This butterfly is mostly orange, with a pattern of black dots, dashes and crescents. Underneath, the hindwing has a row of silver wedges and a row of pale spots around the margin. It flies in woods and heathland.

Species: *Clossiana dia*
Family: Nymphalidae – Size: Up to 34 mm
Flight period: Three; flies between April and August
Distribution: Western Europe eastwards

Small Pearl-bordered Fritillary

This butterfly gets its name from the seven creamy 'pearls' edged in black that run around the margin of the hindwing underside. There is also a large pearl-silver mark towards the hindwing edge, which is important for identification. Above, the wings are orange with a dark pattern of dots, dashes and crescents. This fritillary flies in woodland glades and wet meadows. Its caterpillars feed on violets.

Species: *Boloria selene*
Family: Nymphalidae
Size: Up to 42 mm
Flight period: Two; flies between April and August
Distribution: Western Europe eastwards

Cleopatra

Males of this large butterfly are easy to recognize. They have bright yellow wings, with a large orange area on the forewings. Females, by contrast, have very pale green wings, and could easily be confused with the female brimstone. The Cleopatra flies along waysides and woodland edges, and the caterpillars feed on buckthorn.

Species: *Gonepteryx cleopatra*
Family: Pieridae – Size: Up to 64 mm
Flight period: One; flies between March and August
Distribution: Southern Europe from Spain to the Balkans

Wood White

The Wood White has small, slightly pointed white wings. Males have a grey blob at the forewing tip. The undersides are white, too. In woodland glades and along shady pathways, you may spot the Wood White fluttering feebly, stopping to drink nectar from wild flowers. Caterpillars eat vetch plants and birdsfoot trefoil.

Species: *Leptidea sinapis*
Family: Pieridae
Size: Up to 40 mm
Flight period: Two; flies between May and August
Distribution: Most of Europe

Camberwell Beauty

This is indeed a beautiful butterfly, with big, velvety maroon wings that have broad creamy-yellow borders lined with blue spots. The undersides are similar, but with whitish borders. It was named after the village of Camberwell, now part of London, where it was first found. Camberwell Beauties fly in woodlands, hills and uplands, gliding through treetops or along streams. They are fond of the sun and will sunbathe for hours. Their caterpillars eat willow, beech and elm leaves.

Species: *Nymphalis antiopa*
Family: Nymphalidae
Size: Up to 64 mm
Flight period: One; flies between June and September
Distribution: Most of Europe except southern Spain and Ireland

Northern Chequered Skipper

This butterfly has yellowish forewings with a row of black marks around the margins, and a large central black spot. By contrast, the hindwings are dark brown with orange spots. The Northern Chequered Skipper lives in woodlands and meadows, and can be seen in the summer. Its caterpillars feed on grasses, including dog's tail.

Species: *Carterocephalus silvicolus*
Family: Hesperiidae – Size: Up to 28 mm
Flight period: One; flies between June and July
Distribution: Germany, Poland and Scandinavia

Find Out Some More

Useful organizations

The best organization for you to get in touch with is your local County Wildlife Trust. There are forty-seven of these trusts in Great Britain and you should contact them if you want to know about wildlife and nature reserves and activities in your area. Ask your local library for their address, or contact:

The Wildlife Trusts (previously the Royal Society for Nature Conservation), The Green, Witham Park, Waterside South, Lincoln, LN5 7JR (01522–544400).

Wildlife Watch is the junior branch of The Wildlife Trusts. Local Wildlife Watch groups run meetings all over the country. Again you can find out about your nearest Wildlife Watch group by contacting The Wildlife Trusts.

Your local **natural history society** may organize walks to find and study butterflies. They are led by local experts and you will find them of great help. Your local library will have a list of them.

National Trust for Places of Historic Interest or Natural Beauty, 36 Queen Anne's Gate, London SW1H 9AS (0171–222 9251). They own more than 570 properties and over 232,000 hectares of countryside throughout England, Wales and Northern Ireland. These include many woods, nature reserves and sites of special scientific interest. Most of this is open to visitors, but you usually have to pay to get into a property. The National Trust also run many courses with school groups; ask your teacher to find out about these.

In Scotland, contact **National Trust for Scotland** (care of the Education Adviser), 5 Charlotte Square, Edinburgh EH2 4DU (0131–226 5922).

English Nature (the Nature Conservancy Council for England), Northminster House, Peterborough, Cambs PE1 1UA. (01733–340345) They will send you a list of local nature reserves. Many of these reserves have an interpretive centre to explain the wildlife present there.

In Scotland, contact **Scottish National Heritage**, 12 Hope Terrace, Edinburgh EH9 2AS. (0131–447 4784)

The British Trust for Conservation Volunteers (BTCV), 36 St Mary's Street, Wallingford, Oxon OX10 0EU (01491–39766). They work in partnership with landowner, local communities, councils, businesses and charities to protect and maintain rare habitats, footpaths and nature trails. They publish a quarterly magazine, called *The Conserver*, which keeps members up to date with the latest news. They also have a School Membership Scheme; ask your teacher to find out about this.

Useful books

Butterflies & Moths, David Carter (Dorling Kindersley EYEWITNESS HANDBOOK). Covers 500 species from around the world.

Create Your Own Nature Reserve, Janet Kelly (Simon & Schuster). This is a practical activity book which will show you how to create a nature reserve in your own garden.

Enjoying Wildlife, a guide to RSPB nature reserves, Bob Scott. Updated on a regular basis, this tells you how to find the nature reserves run by the Royal Society for the Protection of Birds around Great Britain, and what you might see there.

Field Guide to the Butterflies and Other Insects of Britain, edited by John Feltwell (Reader's Digest). Wide-ranging guide to the insects of Britain.

Field Guide to Caterpillars of Butterflies and Moths in Britain and Europe, D. Carter & B. Hargreaves (HarperCollins).

Butterflies of Britain and Europe, John Feltwell & Brian Hargreaves (Dragon's World). Spiral-bound pocket guide packed with factual information.

Wildlife Watch Really Useful Insect Pack (Richmond Publishing Co. Ltd).

Index & Glossary

To find the name of a butterfly in this index, search under its main name. So, to look up Southern White Admiral, look under 'Admiral, White' not under Southern or White. The names of butterfly families are shown in **BOLD** type.

Places to visit

Butterflies are part of the enormous insect family, but they are not found as widely as most insects.
One of the best ways to see butterflies is to visit a butterfly farm or sanctuary – ask your local library or tourist authority for information about where they are located.

Many museums have collections of butterflies which you can go and look at. This is worth doing as they won't fly away and so you can look at them in detail. Ask at your local museum or you could try:
British Museum of Natural History, Cromwell Road, London SW7 5BD. (0171–938 9123)
Oxford University Museum, Parks Road, Oxford OX1 3PW. (01865–272950)
National Museum of Wales, Cathays Park, Cardiff CF1 3NP. (01222–397951)
Royal Museum of Scotland, Chambers Street, Edinburgh EH1 1JF. (0131–225 7534)

Index & Glossary